D0160812

AUG 2 5 2008

Meeting the Needs
of Your Most Able Pupils:

MODERN FOREIGN
LANGUAGES

Other titles in the series

Meeting the Needs of Your Most Able Pupils: Art
Kim Earle
1 84312 331 2
978 1 84312 331 6

Meeting the Needs of Your Most Able Pupils: Design and Technology
Louise T. Davies
1 84312 330 4
978 1 84312 330 9

Meeting the Needs of Your Most Able Pupils: English
Erica Glew
1 84312 261 8
978 1 84312 261 6

Meeting the Needs of Your Most Able Pupils: Geography
Jane Ferretti
1 84312 335 5
978 1 84312 335 4

Meeting the Needs of Your Most Able Pupils: History
Steven Barnes
1 84312 287 1
978 1 84312 287 6

Meeting the Needs of Your Most Able Pupils: Mathematics
Lynne McClure and Jennifer Piggott
1 84312 328 2
978 1 84312 328 6

Meeting the Needs of Your Most Able Pupils: Music
Jonathan Savage
1 84312 347 9
978 1 84312 347 7

Meeting the Needs of Your Most Able Pupils: Physical Education and Sport
David Morley and Richard Bailey
1 84312 334 7
978 1 84312 334 7

Meeting the Needs of Your Most Able Pupils: Religious Education
Dilwyn Hunt
1 84312 278 2
978 1 84312 278 4

Meeting the Needs
of Your Most Able Pupils:
MODERN FOREIGN LANGUAGES

Gretchen Ingram

Routledge
Taylor & Francis Group

LONDON AND NEW YORK

First published 2008 by
Routledge
2 Park Square, Milton Park, Abingdon, Oxon OX14 4RN

Simultaneously published in the USA and Canada by
Routledge
270 Madison Ave, New York, NY 10016

Routledge is an imprint of Taylor & Francis, an informa business

Copyright © Gretchen Ingram 2008

British Library Cataloguing in Publication data
A catalogue record for this book is available from the British Library

Library of Congress Cataloging in Publication Data
A catalog record has been requested

ISBN 13: 978 1 84312 332 3 (pbk)
ISBN 13: 978 0 203 93231 5 (ebk)
ISBN 10: 1 84312 332 0 (pbk)
ISBN 10: 0 203 93231 5 (ebk)

All rights reserved. No part of this book may be reprinted or reproduced or utilised in any form or by any electronic, mechanical, or other means, now known or hereafter invented, including photocopying and recording, or in any information storage or retrieval system, without permission in writing from the publishers.

Every effort has been made to contact copyright holders for their permission. The publishers would be grateful to hear from any copyright holder who is not acknowledged here and will undertake to rectify any omissions in future editions of the book. Crown Copyright material is reproduced with the permission of the Controller of HMSO and the Queen's Printer for Scotland.

Series production editors: Sarah Fish and Andrew Welsh
Typeset by Servis Filmsetting Ltd, Manchester
Printed and bound in Great Britain
by Bell & Bain Ltd, Glasgow

To Robert and all my family, for their love and support.

Contents

Acknowledgements

Thanks to Gwen Goodhew for her expert guidance in this demanding project.

Thanks to various fellow professionals: Ursula Badinski, Clare Benson, Sally Benson, Richard and Robert Ingram, Catherine Jones, Becky Lloyd, Carol Annett and Alison Rice.

I am grateful to several experts whose clear and often inspiring writing has helped me improve my understanding of the needs of gifted and talented pupils. They include Deborah Eyre, David George, Joan Freeman, Howard Gardner, Hilary Lowe, Catherine Clark, Ralph Callow, Richard Riding, Susan Leyden and Gwen Goodhew. The work of Ted Wragg and George Brown on questioning is also invaluable.

Finally, I owe thanks to the many gifted and talented people I have worked with and learned from in 25 years of teaching, most recently the TESOL team at Wolverhampton University.

Contributors to the series

The author

Gretchen Ingram is a former head of department with wide experience of teaching, learning and examining modern foreign languages in various UK comprehensive schools.

Series editor

Gwen Goodhew's many and varied roles within the field of gifted and talented education have included school G&T coordinator, director of Wirral Able Children Centre, Knowsley Excellence in Cities (EiC) G&T coordinator, member of the DfES G&T Advisory Group, teacher trainer and consultant. She has written and edited numerous reports and articles on the subject and co-authored *Providing for Able Children* with Linda Evans.

Other authors

Art

Kim Earle is a former secondary head of art and design and is currently an able pupils and arts consultant for St Helens. She has been a member of DfES steering groups, is an Artsmark validator, a subject editor for G&TWISE and a practising designer jeweller and enameller.

Design and Technology

During the writing of the book **Louise T. Davies** was a part-time subject adviser for design and technology at the QCA (Qualifications and Curriculum Authority), and part of the KS3 National Strategy team for the D&T programme. She has authored over 40 D&T books and award-winning multimedia resources. She is currently deputy chief executive of the Design and Technology Association.

English

Erica Glew teaches English throughout the secondary age range to GCSE, AS and A level. She is the gifted and talented coordinator and head of the learning resources centre at the Holy Trinity Church of England secondary school, a specialist comprehensive school in West Sussex. Erica is also an examiner team leader in English Literature at A level.

Geography

Jane Ferretti is a lecturer in education at the University of Sheffield working in initial teacher training. Until 2003 she was head of geography at King Edward VII School, Sheffield, a large 11–18 comprehensive, and was also involved in gifted and talented initiatives at the school and with the local authority. Jane has co-authored a number of A level geography textbooks and a GCSE revision book and is one of the editors of *Wideworld* magazine. She is a member of the Geographical Association and a contributor to their journals *Teaching Geography* and *Geography*.

History

Steven Barnes is a former head of history at a secondary school and Secondary Strategy consultant for the School Improvement Service in Lincolnshire. He has written history exemplifications for Assessment for Learning for the Secondary National Strategy. He is now an assistant head with responsibility for teaching and learning for a school in Lincolnshire.

Mathematics

Lynne McClure is an independent consultant in the field of mathematics education and G&T. She works with teachers and students in schools all over the UK and abroad as well as Warwick, Cambridge, Oxford Brookes and Edinburgh Universities. Lynne edits several maths and education journals.

Jennifer Piggott is a lecturer in mathematics enrichment and communication technology at Cambridge University. She is Director of the NRICH mathematics project and is part of the eastern region coordination team for the NCETM (National Centre for Excellence in the Teaching of Mathematics). Jennifer is an experienced mathematics and ICT teacher.

Music

Jonathan Savage is a senior lecturer in music education at the Institute of Education, Manchester Metropolitan University. Until 2001 he was head of music at Debenham High School, an 11–16 comprehensive school in Suffolk. He is a co-author of a new resource introducing computer game sound design to the Key Stage 3 curriculum (www.sound2game.net) and managing director of UCan.tv (www.ucan.tv), a company specialising in the production of educational software and hardware. When not doing all of this, he is busy parenting four very musically talented children!

Physical Education and Sport

David Morley has taught physical education in a number of secondary schools. He is currently senior lecturer in physical education at Leeds Metropolitan University and the director of the national DfES-funded 'Development in PE' project which is part of the Gifted and Talented strand of the PE, School Sport and Club Links (PESSCL) project. He is also a member of the team responsible for developing resources for national Multi-skill Clubs and is the founder and director of the Carnegie Regional Multi-skill Camp held at Leeds Met Carnegie.

Richard Bailey is professor of pedagogy at Roehampton University, having previously worked at Reading and Leeds Metropolitan University, and at Canterbury Christ Church University where he was director of the Centre for Physical Education Research. He is a well-known author and speaker on physical education, sport and education.

Religious Education

Dilwyn Hunt has worked as a specialist RE adviser in Birmingham and Dudley in the West Midlands, and has a wide range of teaching experience. He is currently a school adviser with responsibility for gifted and talented pupils.

Online content on the Routledge website

The online material accompanying this book may be used by the purchasing individual/organisation only. The files may be amended to suit particular situations, or individual learning needs, and printed out for use by the purchaser. The material can be accessed at www.routledge.com/education/fultonresources.asp

www.routledge.com/education

Introduction

Who should use this book?

This book is for all teachers of modern foreign languages working with Key Stage 3 and Key Stage 4 pupils. It will be relevant to teachers working within the full spectrum of schools, from highly selective establishments to comprehensive and secondary modern schools as well as some special schools. Its overall objective is to provide a practical resource that heads of department, gifted and talented coordinators, leading teachers for gifted and talented education and classroom teachers can use to develop a coherent approach to provision for their most able pupils.

Why is it needed?

School populations differ greatly and pupils considered very able in one setting might not stand out in another. Nevertheless, whatever the general level of ability within a school, there has been a tendency to plan and provide for the middle range, to modify for those who are struggling and to leave the most able to 'get on with it'. This has meant that the most able have:

- not been sufficiently challenged and stimulated

- underachieved

- been unaware of what they might be capable of achieving

- been unaware of what they need to do to achieve at the highest level

- not had high enough ambitions and aspirations

- sometimes become disaffected.

How will this book help teachers?

This book and its accompanying website will, through its combination of practical ideas, materials for photocopying or downloading, and case studies:

- help teachers of MFL to focus on the top 5–10% of the ability range in their particular school and to find ways of providing for these pupils, both within and beyond the classroom

- equip them with strategies and ideas to support exceptionally able pupils, i.e. those in the top 5% nationally.

Terminology

The terms 'more able', 'most able' and 'exceptionally able' will generally be used in this series.

When 'gifted' and 'talented' are used, the definitions provided by the Department for Education and Skills (DfES) in its Excellence in Cities programme will apply. That is:

- **gifted** pupils are the most academically able in a school. This ability might be general or specific to a particular subject area, such as mathematics.

- **talented** pupils are those with high ability or potential in art, music, performing arts or sport.

The two groups together should form 5–10% of any school population.

There are, of course, some pupils who are both gifted and talented. Examples that come to mind are the budding physicist who plays the violin to a high standard in his spare time, or the pupil with high general academic ability who plays for the area football team.

This book is part of a series dealing with providing challenge for the most able secondary age pupils in a range of subjects. It is likely that some of the books in the series might also contain ideas that would be relevant to teachers of MFL.

CHAPTER 1

Our more able pupils – the national scene

- Making good provision for the most able – what's in it for schools?
- National initiatives since 1997
- *Every Child Matters* and the Children Act 2004
- *Higher Standards, Better Schools for All* – Education White Paper, October 2005
- Self-evaluation and inspection
- Resources for teachers and parents of more able pupils

Today's gifted pupils are tomorrow's social, intellectual, economic and cultural leaders and their development cannot be left to chance.

(Deborah Eyre, director of the National Academy for Gifted and Talented Youth, 2004)

The debate about whether to make special provision for the most able pupils in secondary schools ran its course during the last decade of the twentieth century. Explicit provision to meet their learning needs is now considered neither elitist nor a luxury. From an inclusion angle these pupils must have the same chances as others to develop their potential to the full. We know from international research that focusing on the needs of the most able changes teachers' perceptions of the needs of all their pupils, and there follows a consequential rise in standards. But for teachers who are not convinced by the inclusion or school improvement arguments, there is a much more pragmatic reason for meeting the needs of able pupils. Of course, it is preferable that colleagues share a common willingness to address the needs of the most able, but if they don't, it can at least be pointed out that, quite simply, it is something that all teachers are now required to do, not an optional extra.

All schools should seek to create an atmosphere in which to excel is not only acceptable but desirable.

(*Excellence in Schools* – DfEE 1997)

> High achievement is determined by 'the school's commitment to inclusion and the steps it takes to ensure that every pupil does as well as possible'.
>
> (*Handbook for Inspecting Secondary Schools* – Ofsted 2003)

A few years ago, efforts to raise standards in schools concentrated on getting as many pupils as possible over the Level 5 hurdle at the end of Key Stage 3 and over the 5 A*–C grades hurdle at GCSE. Resources were pumped into borderline pupils and the most able were not, on the whole, considered a cause for concern. The situation has changed dramatically in the last nine years with schools being expected to set targets for A*s and As and to show added value by helping pupils entering the school with high SATs scores to achieve Levels 7 and beyond, if supporting data suggests that that is what is achievable. Early recognition of high potential and the setting of curricular targets are at last addressing the lack of progress demonstrated by many able pupils in Year 7 and more attention is being paid to creating a climate in which learning can flourish. But there is a push for even more support for the most able through the promotion of personalised learning.

> The goal is that five years from now: gifted and talented students progress in line with their ability rather than their age; schools inform parents about tailored provision in an annual school profile; curricula include a gifted and talented dimension and at 14–19 there is more stretch and differentiation at the top end, so no matter what your talent it will be engaged; and the effect of poverty on achievement is reduced, because support for high-ability students from poorer backgrounds enables them to thrive.
>
> (Speech at National Academy for Gifted and Talented Youth – David Miliband, Minister for State for School Standards, May 2004)

It is hoped that this book, with the others in this series, will help to accelerate these changes.

Making good provision for the most able – what's in it for schools?

Schools and/or subject departments often approach provision for the most able pupils with some reluctance because they imagine a lot of extra work for very little reward. In fact, the rewards of providing for these pupils are substantial.

- It can be very stimulating to the subject specialist to explore ways of developing approaches with enthusiastic and able students.

> Taking a serious look at what I should expect from the most able and then at how I should teach them has given my teaching a new lease of life. I feel so sorry for youngsters who were taught by me ten years ago. They must have been bored beyond belief. But then, to be quite honest, so was I.
>
> (Science teacher)

- Offering opportunities to tackle work in a more challenging manner often interests pupils whose abilities have gone unnoticed because they have not been motivated by a bland educational diet.

> Some of the others were invited to an after-school maths club. When I heard what they were doing, it sounded so interesting that I asked the maths teacher if I could go too. She was a bit doubtful at first because I have messed about a lot but she agreed to take me on trial. I'm one of her star pupils now and she reckons I'll easily get an A*. I still find some of the lessons really slow and boring but I don't mess around – well, not too much.
>
> (Year 10 boy)

- When pupils are engaged by the work they are doing motivation, attainment and discipline improve.

> You don't need to be gifted to work out that the work we do is much more interesting and exciting. It's made others want to be like us.
> (Comment of a student involved in an extension programme for the most able)

- Schools identified as very good by Ofsted generally have good provision for their most able students.

> If you are willing to deal effectively with the needs of able pupils you will raise the achievement of all pupils.
> (Mike Tomlinson, former director of Ofsted)

- The same is true of individual departments in secondary schools. All those considered to be very good have spent time developing a sound working approach that meets the needs of their most able pupils.

> The department creates a positive atmosphere by its organisation, display and the way that students are valued. Learning is generally very good and often excellent throughout the school. The teachers' high expectations permeate the atmosphere and are a significant factor in raising achievement. These expectations are reflected in the curriculum which has depth and students are able and expected to experience difficult problems in all year groups.
> (Mathematics Department, Hamstead Hall School, Birmingham; Ofsted 2003)

National initiatives since 1997

In 1997, the new government demonstrated its commitment to gifted and talented education by setting up a Gifted and Talented Advisory Group (GTAG). Since then there has been a wide range of government and government-funded initiatives that have, either directly or indirectly, impacted on our most able pupils and their teachers. Details of some can be found below. Others that relate to MFL will be found later in this book.

Excellence in Cities

In an attempt to deal with the chronic underachievement of able pupils in inner city areas, Excellence in Cities (EiC) was launched in 1999. This was a very ambitious, well-funded programme with many different strands. In the first place it concentrated on secondary age pupils but work was extended into the primary sector in many areas. Provision for gifted and talented students was one of the strands.

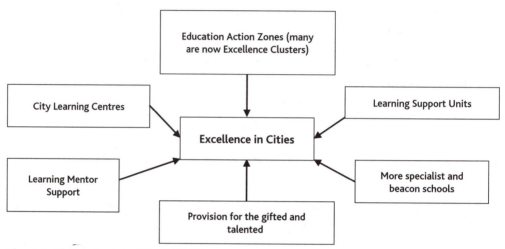

Strands in the Excellence in Cities Initiative

EiC schools were expected to:

- develop a whole-school policy for their most able pupils

- appoint a gifted and talented coordinator with sufficient time to fulfil the role

- send the coordinator on a national training programme run by Oxford Brookes University

- identify 5–10% of pupils in each year group as their gifted and talented cohort, the gifted being the academically able and the talented being those with latent or obvious ability in PE, sport, music, art or the performing arts

- provide an appropriate programme of work both within the school day and beyond

- set 'aspirational' targets both for the gifted and talented cohort as a whole and for individual pupils

- work with other schools in a 'cluster' to provide further support for these pupils

- work with other agencies, such as Aimhigher, universities, businesses and private sector schools, to enhance provision and opportunities for these pupils.

Funding changes have meant that schools no longer receive dedicated EiC money through local authorities but the lessons learned from EiC have been influential in developing a national approach to gifted and talented education. All schools are now expected to adopt similar strategies to ensure that the needs of their most able students are met.

Excellence Clusters

Although EiC was set up initially in the main urban conurbations, other hot spots of underachievement and poverty were also identified and Excellence Clusters were established. For example, Ellesmere Port, Crewe and Barrow-in-Furness are pockets of deprivation, with major social problems and significant underachievement, in otherwise affluent areas. Excellence Clusters have been established in these three places and measures are being taken to improve provision for the most able pupils. The approach is similar to that used in Excellence in Cities areas.

Aimhigher

Aimhigher is another initiative of the Department for Education and Skills (DfES) working in partnership with the Higher Education Funding Council for England (HEFCE). Its remit is to widen participation in UK higher education, particularly among students from groups that do not have a tradition of going to university, such as some ethnic minorities, the disabled and those from poorer homes. Both higher education institutions and secondary schools have Aimhigher coordinators who work together to identify pupils who would benefit from additional support and to plan a programme of activities. Opportunities are likely to include:

- mentoring, including e-mentoring
- residential summer schools
- visits to different campuses and university departments
- masterclasses
- online information for students and parents
- advice on the wide range of financial and other support available to disadvantaged students.

One national Aimhigher project, Higher Education Gateway, is specifically targeted on gifted and talented students from disadvantaged groups. More information can be found at www.aimhigher.ac.uk.

National Academy for Gifted and Talented Youth (NAGTY)

Government initiatives have not been confined to the most able pupils in deprived areas. In 2002, the National Academy for Gifted and Talented Youth was established at Warwick University. Its brief was to offer support to the most able 5% of the school population and their teachers and parents. It did this in a number of ways:

National Academy for Gifted and Talented Youth		
Student Academy	**Professional Academy**	**Expertise Centre**
• Summer schools including link-ups with CTY in USA. • Outreach courses in a wide range of subjects at universities and other venues across the country. • Online activities – currently maths, classics, ethics, philosophy.	• Continuing professional development for teachers. • A PGCE+ programme for trainee teachers. • Ambassador School Programme to disseminate good practice amongst schools.	• Leading research in gifted and talented education.

NAGTY worked closely with the DfES with the latter setting policy and NAGTY increasingly taking the lead in the practical application of this policy – a policy known as the English Model, which, as explained on NAGTY's website, is 'rooted in day-to-day classroom provision and enhanced by additional, more advanced opportunities offered both within school and outside of it'. NAGTY ceased operation in August 2007 and was replaced by the Young, Gifted & Talented Programme (see below).

The Young, Gifted & Talented Programme (YG&T)

In December 2006, the UK government announced the creation of a new programme in England, the National Programme for Gifted and Talented Education (NPGATE), to be managed by CfBT Education Trust and now known as the Young, Gifted & Talented Programme (YG&T). Among the changes proposed are:

- a much greater emphasis on school and local level provision.

- the setting-up of Excellence Hubs – HEI-led partnerships to provide non-residential summer schools and a diverse range of outreach provision, including summer activities, weekend events and online and blended learning models. There will be free places for the disadvantaged.

Meeting the Needs of Your Most Able Pupils: MODERN FOREIGN LANGUAGES

- the appointment of gifted and talented leading teachers – one for each secondary school and each cluster of primary schools.

- a national training programme for gifted and talented leading teachers organised by the national primary and secondary strategies.

Further information about YG&T can be found at www.dfes.gov.uk/ygt and www.cfbt.com.

Gifted and talented summer schools

Education authorities are encouraged to work in partnership with schools to run a number of summer schools (dependent on the size of the authority) for the most able pupils in Years 6–11. It is expected that there will be a particular emphasis on transition and that around 50 hours of tuition will be offered. Some schools and authorities run summer schools for up to ten days whilst others cover a shorter period and have follow-up sessions or even residential weekends later in the school year. Obviously the main aim is to challenge and stimulate these pupils but the DfES also hopes that:

- they will encourage teachers and advisers to adopt innovative teaching approaches

- teachers will continue to monitor these pupils over time

- where Year 6 pupils are involved, it will make secondary teachers aware of what they can achieve and raise their expectations of Year 7 pupils.

More can be found out about these summer schools at www.standards.dfes.gov.uk/giftedandtalented. Funding for them has now been incorporated into the school development grant.

Regional partnerships

When Excellence in Cities (EiC) was first introduced, gifted and talented strand coordinators from different EiC partnerships began to meet up with others in their regions to explore ways of working together so that the task would be more manageable and resources could be pooled. One of the most successful examples of cooperation was the Trans-Pennine Group that started up in the northwest. It began to organise training on a regional basis as well as masterclasses and other activities for some gifted and talented pupils. The success of this and other groups led to the setting-up of nine regional partnerships with initial support from NAGTY and finance from DfES. Each partnership had a steering group composed of representatives from local authorities, higher education institutions, regional organisations concerned with gifted and talented children and NAGTY. Each regional partnership organised professional training; sought to support schools and areas in greatest need; tried to ensure that all 11- to 19-year-olds who fell into the top 5% of the ability range were registered with NAGTY; provided opportunities for practitioner research and arranged challenging activities for pupils. Under the YG&T Programme, nine Excellence Hubs have been created to continue and expand the work of the regional partnerships.

Every Child Matters: Change for Children and the Children Act 2004

The likelihood of all children reaching their potential has always been hampered by the fragmented nature of agencies concerned with provision for them. Vital information held by an agency about a child's needs has often been kept back from other agencies, including schools. This has had a particularly negative impact on the disadvantaged, for example, looked-after children. In 2004, 57% of looked-after children left school without even one GCSE or GNVQ and only 6% achieved five or more good GCSEs (see national statistics at www.dfes.gov.uk/ rsgateway/). This represents a huge waste of national talent as well as many personal tragedies.

The Children Act 2004 sought to overcome these problems by, amongst other things, requiring:

- local authorities to make arrangements to promote cooperation between agencies to ensure the well-being of all children

- all children's services to bear these five outcomes in mind when planning provision. Children should:
  - be healthy
  - stay safe
  - enjoy and achieve
  - make a positive contribution
  - achieve economic well-being.

There are major implications for schools in seeking to achieve these outcomes for their most able pupils, especially where there is deprivation and/or low aspiration:

- local authorities to appoint a director of children's services to coordinate education and social services

- each local authority to take on the role of corporate parent to promote the educational achievement of looked-after children. This should help to ensure that greater consideration is given to their education when changes in foster placements are being considered

- the setting-up of an integrated inspection regime to look at the totality of provision for children.

More information can be found at www.everychildmatters.gov.uk.

Higher Standards, Better Schools for All (Education White Paper, October 2005)

Although the thrust of this Education White Paper is to improve educational opportunities for all, there is no doubt that some proposals will particularly benefit the most able, especially those that are disadvantaged in some way.

- Pupils receiving free school meals will be able to get **free public transport** to any one of three secondary schools closest to their homes between two and six miles away. At present, such children have very little choice in secondary schooling because their parents cannot afford the fares. This measure will allow them access to schools that might be better able to cater for their particular strengths and needs.

- **The National Register of Gifted and Talented Learners** will record the top 5% of the nation's children, as identified by a wide range of measures, so that they can be tracked and supported throughout their school careers. At first, the focus will be on 11- to 19-year-olds but later identification will start at the age of 4. As a first step, in 2006 all secondary schools were asked to identify gifted and talented students in the school census. In reality, some authorities had already begun this monitoring process but making it a national priority will bring other schools and authorities up to speed.

- In line with new school managerial structures, **'leading teachers' of the gifted and talented** will take the place of gifted and talented coordinators. Training (optionally accredited) will be organised through the national strategies. Leading teachers will work closely with School Improvement Partners and local authority coordinators to implement G& T improvement plans, and undertake much of the work previously undertaken by school coordinators.

- **Additional training** in providing for gifted and talented pupils will be available to all schools.

- **A national programme of non-residential summer schools** will be organised to run alongside gifted and talented summer schools already provided by local authorities and individual schools.

- Secondary schools will be encouraged to make greater use of **grouping by ability** in order to meet the needs of the most able and to use **curriculum flexibility** to allow pupils to take Key Stage 3 tests and GCSE courses early and to mix academic and vocational courses.

- **At advanced level, a new extended project** will allow the most able students to demonstrate high scholastic ability.

- **Extended schools** (see later section).

- **More personalised learning** (see later section).

More information on *Higher Standards, Better Schools for All* can be found at www.dfes.gov.uk/publications/schoolswhitepaper.

Extended schools

In many parts of the country, extended schools are already operating, but it is intended that schools will become much more central in providing a wide range of services to children, parents and the community. The government intends to spend £680 million by 2008 to facilitate these developments. Ideally these services should include:

- all-year childcare from 8.00am to 6.00pm

- referral to a wide range of support services, such as speech therapy, mental health and behaviour support

- exciting activities, including study support and extension/enrichment activities that will motivate the most able

- parenting support, which might include classes on healthy eating, helping children with homework, dealing with challenging behaviour etc

- community use of school facilities, especially ICT.

Again, this is an initiative that will benefit all children, especially those whose carers work. However, there are particular benefits for those children whose school performance suffers because they have nowhere to study at home and for those with talents that parents cannot nurture because of limited means.

More information on Extended Schools can be found at www.teachernet.gov.uk/settingup and www.tda.gov.uk/remodelling/extendedschools.aspx.

Personalised learning

As mentioned earlier in this chapter, a key component of current education reforms is the emphasis on personalised learning – maximising potential by tailoring education to individual needs, strengths and interests. The key features of personalised learning are:

- **Assessment for Learning** – Information from data and the tasks and assessments pupils undertake must be used to feed back suggestions about how work could be improved and what learning they need to do next. But the feedback should be a two-way process with pupils also providing information to teachers about factors impeding their learning and approaches that would enhance it. This feedback should inform future lesson planning. For the most able pupils, effective assessment for learning should mean that they move forward with their learning at an appropriate pace and depth, rather than marking time while others catch up.

- **Effective Teaching and Learning Strategies** – It is still the case that many teachers teach only in the way that was most successful for them as learners. There is ample evidence that our most able pupils do not form an homogeneous group and that, in order to bring out their many and varied gifts and talents, we need to adopt a wide range of teaching strategies, making full use of the opportunities provided by ICT. At the same time pupils need to become aware of the learning strategies that are most successful for them, whilst also exploring a broader range of learning approaches.

- **Curriculum Entitlement and Choice** – There are many examples of highly gifted adults whose abilities were masked at school because the curriculum did not appear to be relevant to them. Schools need to take the opportunities afforded by new flexibility in the curriculum, by the specialised diplomas of study being introduced for 14- to 19-year-olds and by partnership with other schools, colleges and businesses to engage their pupils. There are several schools now where more able pupils cover Key Stage 3 in two years. The year that is freed up by this approach can be used in a variety of ways, such as starting GCSE courses early, following an enrichment programme or taking up additional science and language courses. The possibilities are endless if there is desire for change.

- **School Organisation** – Effective personalisation demands a more flexible approach to school organisation. This flexibility might show itself in the way teaching and support staff are deployed, by the way pupils are grouped, by the structure of the school day and by the way in which ICT is used to enable learning to take place beyond the classroom. At least one school is abandoning grouping by age in favour of grouping by ability in the hope that this will provide the necessary challenge for the most able. It remains to be seen how successful this approach is but experimentation and risk-taking is essential if we are to make schooling relevant and exciting for our most able pupils.

- **Partnerships Beyond Schools** – Schools cannot provide adequately for their most able pupils without making full use of the opportunities and expertise offered by other groups within the community, including parents together with family support groups, social and health services, sports clubs and other recreational and business organisations.

The websites www.standards.dfes.gov.uk/personalisedlearning and www.teachernet.gov.uk/publications/ will provide more information on personalised learning, whilst new curriculum opportunities to be offered to 14- to 19-year-olds are described in www.dfes.gov.uk/14-19.

Self-evaluation and inspection

The most able must have as many opportunities for development as other pupils. Poor, unchallenging teaching or an ideology that confuses equality of opportunity with levelling down should not hinder their progress. They should have a fair share of a school's resources both in terms of learning materials and in human resources. The environment for learning should be one in which it is safe to be clever and to excel. These are points that schools should consider when preparing their self-evaluation and school development plans.

There have been dramatic changes in the relationships between schools and local authorities and in the schools' inspection regime since the Children Act 2004. Local authorities are now regarded as commissioners for services for children. One of their tasks is to facilitate the appointment of SIPs, School Improvement Partners, who act as the main conduit between schools and LAs and take part in an 'annual conversation' with their schools when the school's self-evaluation and progress towards targets is discussed.

Self-evaluation is also the cornerstone of the new shorter, more frequent Ofsted inspections, using a SEF (self-evaluation form) as a central point of reference together with the five outcomes for children of *Every Child Matters*. An invaluable tool for schools recognising that they need to do more for their gifted and talented pupils, or simply wanting to assess their current provision, is the institutional quality standards for gifted and talented education (IQS).

Institutional quality standards for gifted and talented education (IQS)

These standards, developed by a partnership of the DfES, NAGTY and other interested groups, are an essential self-evaluation tool for any school focusing on its gifted and talented provision. Under each of five headings, schools look carefully at the level indicators and decide which of the three levels they have achieved:

- **Entry level** – a school making its first steps towards developing a whole school policy might find that much of its provision falls into this category. Ofsted would rate such provision satisfactory.

- **Developing level** – where there is some effective practice but there is room for development and improvement. This aligns with a good from Ofsted.

- **Exemplary level** – where good practice is exceptional and sustained. Ofsted would rate this excellent.

The five headings show clear links to the personalisation agenda: effective teaching and learning strategies; enabling curriculum entitlement and choice; assessment for learning; school organisation; and strong partnerships beyond school.

Having identified the levels at which they are performing, schools are then able to draw up development plans. A copy of these standards is included in the appendices and more information about them can be found at www2. teachernet.gov.uk/qualitystandards.

Resources for teachers and parents of more able pupils

There is currently an abundance of resources and support agencies for teachers, parents and gifted and talented young people themselves. A few of general interest are included below. Other MFL education examples will be found in later chapters of this book.

World Class Tests

These have been introduced by QCA to allow schools to judge the performance of their most able pupils against national and international standards. Currently tests are available for 9- and 13-year-olds in mathematics and problem solving. Some schools have found that the problem solving tests are effective at identifying able underachievers in maths and science. The website contains sample questions so that teachers, parents and pupils themselves can assess the tests' suitability for particular pupils or groups of pupils, and the tests themselves are also available online. For more information go to www.worldclassarena.org.uk.

National Curriculum Online

This website, administered by QCA, provides general guidance on all aspects of the national curriculum but also has a substantial section on general and subject-specific issues relating to gifted and talented education, including identification strategies, case studies, management and units of work. Details of the National Curriculum Online can be found at www.nc.uk.net/gt.

G&TWise

G&TWise links to recommended resources for gifted and talented pupils, checked by professionally qualified subject editors, in all subjects and at all key stages and provides up-to-date information for teachers on gifted and talented education. Details can be found at www2.teachernet.gov.uk.

NACE – the National Association for Able Children in Education

NACE is an independent organisation that offers support for teachers and other professionals trying to develop provision for gifted and talented pupils. It gives advice and guidance to teachers and others, runs courses and conferences, provides consultants and keynote speakers.

It has also produced the NACE Challenge Award Framework, which it recommends could be used alongside IQS, as it exemplifies evidence and action planning. While IQS indicates what needs to be improved, the Challenge Award

Framework suggests how to effect change. More information can be found at www.nace.co.uk.

National Association for Gifted Children (NAGC)

NAGC is a charity providing support for gifted and talented children and young people and their parents and teachers. It has a regional structure and in some parts of the country there are branch activities for children and parents. NAGC provides: counselling for both young people and their parents; INSET and courses for teachers; publications; activities for 3- to 10-year-olds; and a dedicated area on its website for 11- to 19-year-olds (to which they have exclusive access), called Youth Agency. For further information go to www.nagcbritain. org.uk.

Children of High Intelligence (CHI)

CHI acts on behalf of children whose intelligence puts them above the 98th percentile. It often acts in a support capacity when parents are negotiating appropriate provision with schools and local authorities. For further details visit www.chi-charity.org.uk.

Summary

- Schools must provide suitable challenge and support for their most able pupils.
- Appropriate provision can enhance motivation and improve behaviour.
- Recent legislation to support disadvantaged children should mean that fewer potentially gifted and talented children fall through the net.
- Effective self-evaluation of school provision for gifted and talented pupils and challenging targets are the keys to progress.
- There are many agencies that can help teachers with this work.

CHAPTER 2

Departmental policy and approach

- The role of the subject leader
- Making a start: auditing provision for the most able pupils in MFL at Key Stage 3/4
- Formulating departmental policy
- Grouping policy, acceleration and collaborative learning
- Allocation of resources
- Liaison with other departments
- Monitoring and assessment
- INSET activities for the department

This chapter will map out how teachers within the modern foreign languages (MFL) department can work together to devise their strategy for meeting the needs of its more able pupils, with suggested guidelines for those who will lead the process.

As with many of the central activities in teaching and learning, the process is as important as the outcome. It is an opportunity for teachers to formulate their thinking: the more that individual teachers are able to contribute, the more they will 'own' the resulting working document.

The role of the subject leader

The Teacher Training Agency (TTA), now the Training and Development Agency (TDA), outlined the key responsibilities of the subject leader/head of department (HOD). S/he is ultimately responsible for the teaching and learning of all pupils in MFL. However, HODs can, where appropriate, devolve responsibilities and delegate tasks to other teachers.

The National Standards for Subject Leaders

National Standards for Subject Leaders were set out by the TTA (now known as TDA), to define clear expectations and recognise teachers' expertise. Although the framework has been revised, it is worth looking at the list of expectations that would most affect the more able cohort. To ensure that the department improves provision for these pupils, the subject leader would work to:

- develop and implement policies and practices for the subject which reflect the school's commitment to high achievement, effective teaching and learning
- use data effectively to identify pupils who are underachieving in the subject and, where necessary, create and implement effective plans of action to support those pupils
- analyse and interpret relevant national, local and school data, plus research and inspection evidence, to inform policies, practices, expectations, targets and teaching methods
- establish, with the involvement of relevant staff, short-, medium- and long-term plans for the development and resourcing of the subject, which:
    - are based on a range of comparative information and evidence, including in relation to the attainment of pupils
    - identify realistic and challenging targets for improvement in the subject
    - are understood by all those involved in putting the plans into practice
    - are clear about action to be taken, timescales and criteria for success
- monitor the progress made in achieving subject plans and targets, evaluate the effects on teaching and learning, and use this analysis to guide further improvement.

The subject leader would also:

- ensure curriculum coverage, continuity and progression in the subject for all pupils, including those of high ability and those with special educational or linguistic needs
- provide guidance on the choice of appropriate teaching and learning methods to meet the needs of the subject and of different pupils
- establish and implement clear policies and practices for assessing, recording and reporting on pupil achievement, and for using this information to recognise achievement and to assist pupils in setting targets for further improvement
- ensure that information about pupils' achievements in previous classes and schools is used effectively to secure good progress in the subject
- evaluate the teaching of the subject in the school, use this analysis to identify effective practice and areas for improvement, and take action to improve further the quality of teaching
- establish clear expectations and constructive working relationships among staff involved with the subject, including through team working and mutual support; devolving responsibilities and delegating tasks, as appropriate; evaluating practice; and developing an acceptance of accountability
- audit training needs of subject staff

- lead professional development of subject staff through example and support, and coordinate the provision of high quality professional development by methods such as coaching, drawing on other sources of expertise as necessary, for example, higher education, LAs, subject associations
- enable teachers to achieve expertise in their subject teaching
- establish staff and resource needs for the subject.

Depending on resources and size of the school, as well as the size of the MFL department, a school could nominate another member of the department as a gifted and talented coordinator or representative. The job description given below is a list to help focus thinking about the role. In many schools the description will simply apply to the head of department, wearing their 'responsible for the more able' hat.

The department does not work in a vacuum. The Key Stage 3 National Strategy points to whole-school values to be developed within which second language-learning is valued and can flourish: not just for examination results, but for its long-term – even lifetime – benefits.

Before looking at how, we look at what needs to be done. The key responsibilities for the school gifted and talented coordinator have been set out by the DfES. The department representative will liaise between the school coordinator and the department. This draft description (included on the website) could be adapted to cover a suitable range of responsibilities and tasks.

Job description for a person with responsibility for more able pupils within the MFL department

1. General

To support school provision of opportunities to develop the skills, abilities and talents of the most able pupils to the full – to take up their cause.

2. Policy

To contribute to the development of school and department policy on identification, teaching and learning of more able pupils as well as the implementation, monitoring and evaluation of that policy.

3. The identification process

To work with the department staff to define what they mean by 'most able' and to identify their most able pupils, using, for example:

- MFL teachers' records and nominations
- feeder schools' data
- information from the school G&T coordinator
- parents and pupils
- pastoral heads, where pastoral support and/or counselling may be necessary
- form tutors.

4. Organisation

Along with the head of department:

- to work through the setting and grouping process with reference to the most able pupils

- to consider acceleration, fast tracking or early entry for the most able pupils

- to set up measures to monitor and support the progress of the most able pupils.

5. Lessons

- To assist/lead/promote department training in ways of providing suitable programmes for the most able pupils, to take account of:

  - embedding extension activities and enrichment in schemes of work and lesson plans

  - developing thinking skills required for MFL

  - individual learning styles of pupils

  - homework and independent learning

  - assessment (formative and summative)

  - promoting a positive learning climate

  - coordinating dissemination of good practice within the department.

- To keep abreast of national and local developments and brief the department (for example, as an item on regular departmental meeting agenda).

- To liaise with the local authority (LA) adviser over continuing professional development (CPD) with the department, to disseminate information over opportunities and with coordinators in other departments, where appropriate.

- To encourage colleagues to join working groups and take up relevant training.

6. Out of class

- To brief department on provision, especially what is offered externally: competitions, courses, other activities, masterclasses.

- To lead an after-school languages club, or similar out-of-class activity.

- To develop suitable study support for the most able.

- To liaise with the LA G&T coordinator for MFL.

- To liaise with other schools and colleges within the consortium.

7. Transfer between schools

To support pupils as they move on to higher courses in other schools and colleges.

8. Resources, including ICT

- To assist with selection of mentors.

- To assist with the choice of resources.

- To liaise with the library/learning base.

9. Monitoring and evaluation

- With the HOD, devising means of monitoring G&T provision (for example, using questionnaires).
- To assist the head of department in carrying out evaluations of department methodology and provision for more able pupils.
- To assist with monitoring progress of more able pupils.
- To help the HOD draw up an action plan.

Making a start: auditing provision for the most able pupils in MFL at Key Stage 3/4

Many schools will have used the subject audit that accompanies the Key Stage 3 National Strategy. Appendix 2.1 is an audit tool using some of the strategies included in that document as well as others relating directly to provision for the most able. An MFL department seeking to improve provision for its most able students must carry out a thorough analysis of current levels of achievement among different groups of potentially able students. This will help to identify the factors that contribute to enthusiasm and high achievement as well as those associated with underachievement or apathy.

Having carried out the audit, the department's next step is to identify a small number of key issues that need to be addressed and draw up a plan of action. See Appendix 2.2 for an action plan grid.

Formulating departmental policy

What to include in a more able or gifted and talented subject policy

It is not essential to have a separate policy for gifted and talented pupils, although some departments do. Others incorporate it into their general departmental document. The subject policy should follow the same framework as the school policy and fit in with its general philosophy. It must also accord with LA policy. A good policy will develop from:

- a thorough and honest audit of existing levels of achievement of the most able and of their attitudes to learning
- clear identification of where changes need to be made and the drawing up of an action plan
- consultation with senior management, gifted and talented coordinator, other staff in the department and pupils
- the existence of effective strategies to monitor and evaluate the measures taken.

Below is a list of headings which might be used when preparing a departmental or subject policy, along with sample statements which can be adapted for an individual department:

1. Policy rationale and aims

- How does the policy relate to the school's overall aims and values?

- How does the subject contribute to the young person's academic and personal development?

- What does the department aim to provide for the most able students?

Example

Working in accordance with the aims of the school and its policy for more able and talented pupils, all teachers in the MFL department are committed to raising the achievement of the more able and talented pupils, in the belief that this will benefit all pupils.

2. Definitions

In the context of your school and subject what do you mean by most able or gifted and/or talented?

Example

Within the school, the gifted and talented pupils are identified as 5% of the population. These pupils are identified in the electronic mark book on the school intranet. Within the department, we define our 'own' cohort, which may vary between 5 and 10% of a year group and must reflect the makeup of the school population as a whole.

3. Identification

- How does your department's approach fit in with the school's practice on identification?

- What subject-specific identification strategies will you use?

Example

In line with school policy we will use the list of pupils identified at whole-school level by objective tests and primary school teacher assessments/recommendations. We will also consider:

- any pupil of high all-round ability or high ability in English
- pupils identified as more able by other departments
- parent/carer information
- pupils' self-nominations and peer nominations

- bilingual pupils
- pupils with direct access to cultures and languages other than English.

By the end of January each year, we will draft our own list of Year 7 pupils and update our lists for other year groups.

4. Organisational issues

- How will teaching groups be organised to meet the needs of all pupils including the most able?

- Will fast tracking, early entry or acceleration to an older age group be considered and what measure will be taken both to support these pupils and to ensure that they continue to make progress?

Example

We will set pupils from Year 8 to Year 11, according to their ability in MFL. Although the more able pupils will therefore be in the top set, that set will nevertheless contain a wide range of ability which will need to be catered for by differentiated work.

The Years 7 and 8 scheme of work will explicitly stress the development of grammatical competence and more rapid progress in French, to allow the most able pupils to reach the highest levels and for a second foreign language to be studied in Years 9, 10 and 11.

Early entry for GCSE will be considered on an individual basis, with input from all concerned: pupil, parents/carers, MFL staff and the pastoral team. For example, the department has agreed with a French-speaking parent that her son will prepare for GCSE French independently and will study only German in school.

5. Provision in lessons

- How do schemes of work and lesson plans reflect the demands to be made of the most able students?

- How will the need for faster pace, more breadth and greater depth in the subject be met?

- How are the thinking skills needed for this subject to be developed?

- How will different learning styles of pupils be catered for?

- How will homework and independent learning be used to enhance their education?

- How is assessment, both formative and summative, used to enable suitable targets to be set and appropriate progress to be made?

- How does the learning climate within the classroom support and encourage the most able?

Example

The department is collaborating to examine and refine the scheme of work to ensure it will provide challenge for its more able pupils. It will provide suitably differentiated work for these pupils, offer opportunities for group work and independent learning and cater for a range of pupils' learning styles. Specific activities will encourage pupils to reflect on their learning and how to extend it.

Certain homework tasks will be designed to offer opportunities for high quality work and use of higher order thinking skills.

In accordance with school policy, certain assessment tasks will have a challenging element aimed at the more able. Feedback from these will be recorded and reviewed each term in order to reward success and/or detect any pattern of underachievement.

Reports will make it clear to parents/carers whether the pupil is/is not meeting high levels of challenge successfully and suggest suitable targets.

6. Out-of-class activities

● What out-of-class activities and study support are offered to the more able?

● How do out-of-class activities and study support relate to provision in lessons?

● Does the department collaborate with outside agencies to benefit the more able?

Example

The department will aim to support the more able pupils outside the classroom through:

● the after-school French club for Year 7 and the Spanish club for Year 9

● the grammar clinic

● the short evening course on 'How to organise a family camping trip to Europe' for pupils and their families

● the intensive language days for Year 7 and 8 pupils.

Pupils who have attended summer school have written about their experience on the school website and have reported back to some of their peers in lessons and assemblies.

7. Transfer and transition

● How is information from primary schools used to ensure progression?

● What measures are taken to assist the most able pupils during their transition from primary to secondary school?

● How are students who move on to sixth forms in other schools or colleges supported?

Example

Years 6–7

The department is liaising with feeder schools which offer a modern foreign language. Year 6 pupils will bring an example of their best work with them during induction week. They will also bring a portfolio to their first MFL lesson, which will be left temporarily for their Year 7 teacher to consult. During induction week, pupils will be given a list of resources and a sample holiday project. This will include online vocabulary-learning games and an open-ended project 'Where does the French language come from?' There will be a prize (probably a piece of language software, or a dictionary, if appropriate) for the best 'answer' to this question. Answers (in English) can be in various forms: using pictures, diagrams or a PowerPoint presentation although entries will be judged more on content than on presentation. The local public library also has the list of resources – in case pupils do not have online access at home.

Years 12, 13 and beyond

All our students can use the University Learning Centre. They will visit the Centre in Year 12 and be shown around by library and MFL staff. Visits to university Open Days will be encouraged. In preparation for these visits, MFL staff will help students prepare questions and ensure that their students have accessed reading lists and found out about study support for the courses they wish to follow. Whenever possible, one of the school's former pupils will visit the group to answer questions about their experience of higher education in MFL.

8. Resources

- How are teaching assistants, learning mentors and other adult helpers used to support the most able?

- What outside agencies are used?

- What specific learning resources are available for the most able?

- How is ICT used to enhance the education of the most able?

Example

The foreign language assistants (FLAs) will be used flexibly to support group work and individual needs and to provide extra resources for special projects.

In consultation with the school coordinator, the department will liaise with the university to match up individual mentors for pupils with special talents (not necessarily the linguistically able) with European university students studying music, sport sciences, performing arts, fine art and design. Consideration will also be given to high achievers in other subjects, such as science, who would benefit from working with a native speaker of the language they are studying, and interested in science.

In-class support is also offered by sixth form language students.

The school library and learning centre has a section of reading and video materials, dictionaries, music CDs and CD-ROMs for more able linguists. The department plans to contribute items to this collection each year. Pupils in Years 7,

8 and 9 have a scheduled visit to the learning centre with a carousel of activities to perform using these resources. The school website has lists of suitable resources and links to helpful sites. Pupils are encouraged to help keep the department's list of sites up to date and to provide brief comments on why a particular site was useful or interesting for them.

9. Monitoring and evaluation

- Who is responsible for liaising with the school coordinator and developing good practice for the most able in your department?

- How is the effectiveness of this policy to be measured?

- What targets does the department have for its most able students (e.g. Levels 7 and 8 at Key Stage 3, A* and A at GCSE)?

- How and when is the progress of individual students and groups monitored?

- What continuing professional development (CPD) is needed or will be provided from colleagues?

Example

Training needs and requests for training will be considered in line with the department and school improvement plan. The department handbook will contain a record of training undertaken, paired observation work and expertise gained on courses and visits, updated annually.

10. Recognition and reward
How will pupil and teacher success be recognised and rewarded?

Example

In line with school policy on rewards, the individual achievements of more able pupils will be recognised. Recommendations will be made for the head teacher's commendation board.
   Teachers, like many professionals, often notice what does not work more than what does. Therefore, in this very complex and demanding job, we will make an effort to share our successes!

Grouping policy, acceleration and collaborative learning

Eyre (1997: 105–107) has a good comparison of four grouping systems and makes the point that organisation in itself does not ensure provision. A well-planned mixed-ability system is better than a setted one which is whole-class taught.

Setting

Most MFL departments use setting: grouping according to achievement in the subject. This allows more able pupils to work at a faster pace. It also puts them in an environment where success is usually acceptable. One of the disadvantages is that, once setting has been done, it is difficult to make changes, and sets tend to remain fixed from one year to the next. This is an argument for working hard to improve the department's awareness and consensus on what constitutes giftedness in their subject. Giving opportunities for pupils in all sets to achieve, using planned differentiation, becomes essential in case potential has been overlooked. Experience and practice will increase teachers' skills in both identification and provision.

Mixed-ability teaching

In a department where all teachers are language specialists as well as excellent practitioners, with planned differentiation for the most able, mixed-ability could be argued to be the best system. However:

> Some very good teachers can successfully extend their most able within a mixed-ability context. It takes careful planning and monitoring, but it can be done. It is, however, very demanding and whilst teachers often say that it is the fairest system, poor mixed-ability teaching is deadly for able pupils. They are demotivated by a slow pace and inhibited from doing well by adverse comments from other pupils. Teachers often rely on their most able pupils to get on alone so that they have time to deal with others. Able pupils get very little teacher time in poorly taught, mixed-ability lessons and underachievement often occurs.
>
> (Eyre 1997: 106)

The above points are particularly relevant for the first year that pupils begin to learn a modern foreign language. They are not likely to be arranged in sets until MFL teachers have had a chance to assess them. Chapter 3 deals with strategies to help teachers to develop their professional competence in identifying the more able. But the scheme of work will have to provide opportunities which allow staff and pupils to become aware of particular strengths.

Acceleration

Acceleration is normally the term used to refer to moving an individual up a year or more. With greater flexibility at Key Stages 3 and 4, the learning needs of particularly able individuals could be met without their having to be separated from their peers. Adolescence is a tricky time to be moving out of one's age/peer group. However, for those who are considering accelerating an individual pupil, a checklist to be used by teachers and parents is included as Appendix 2.3.

Fast tracking

In this system, pupils or groups of pupils move through the programme of study at a rate which allows them to be entered earlier for public examinations. For an individual, or for a small group, this is rarely the best solution unless a great deal of thought has been given to how these pupils are provided for after they have completed the examination. One school's answer is to offer two languages to a 'more able' group, with early entry for one of the languages. The question of early entry for examinations should be considered in a holistic way and in consultation with pupils, parent/carers and teachers in other departments. With the current emphasis on the need for high grades, some pupils and their parent/guardians will be reluctant to compromise the chance of the highest grade. The pupil may already have a heavy programme, with time-consuming out-of-school activities: for example, music examinations, athletic competitions, chess tournaments. In such cases, raising a pupil's competence, confidence and motivation in MFL learning can be combined with those other interests. Travel or study abroad, access to speakers of other languages, international events – these are examples of opportunities which can be used to learn in and through a modern foreign language.

Fast tracking a whole class is another option. Working through Key Stage 3 in two years would allow the class to embark on their GCSE programme a year early. Rather than working relentlessly towards examination performance (and on practising past papers), the group would have an opportunity to read and listen to more varied materials on a wider range of subjects. Their productive skills would have a chance to 'catch up' and reach levels more in keeping with what they are able to say and write in subjects such as English, History and RE. They could begin some AS level work, thereby getting a head start on closing the well-known gap between the demands of GCSE and AS level. Apart from challenging pupils, this could encourage them to continue the subject at A level.

Some schools have even entered carefully selected groups of pupils for GCSE in Year 9, with excellent results. The pupils have then covered AS level in Key Stage 4. In Gosforth High School, pupils were entered for French GCSE in Year 10 (Balmer 2002). They went on to a specially developed course, studying, for example, French music and film and current affairs in two francophone countries.

Another option is to offer a two-year GCSE in another language (say Italian) to pupils who have already passed GCSE French or German in Year 9.

Bilingual pupils, given support to develop their grammatical competence and their writing skills to a high level, could be considered for early entry at GCSE level. These pupils usually have good listening and speaking skills, though they may need to develop their reading skills. Using more challenging texts, they can practise summarising, drawing inferences, even translating. These are transferable skills which will enhance their overall linguistic competence. They can be given appointments with a foreign language assistant or mentor from a higher class to work on grammar, or attend a grammar clinic with a member of the department with particular interest or expertise in this area.

Streaming

In this system, pupils are grouped according to their overall achievement. No account is taken of the difference between all-round ability and exceptional abilities in other areas. It is unlikely that a group identified as more able in MFL – or indeed many other subjects – will correspond with those selected for their all-round ability. Whole-school policy may be to stream and not to set. School size may dictate such a system. In this case, a group of pupils could meet at a time outside the normal school day to pursue a specific programme (see Chapter 6 for examples), while the same pupils undertake enrichment and extension tasks in class time.

Streaming will probably disadvantage the able pupil whose first language is not English.

Case study

Amy had arrived from Hong Kong speaking no English, and in a short time joined a Year 7 group. In an informal staffroom discussion, a colleague in the English department was describing how difficult it was to assess Amy's English when she had no idea about how tenses worked. In French, Amy was an outstanding pupil. She had been learning French on an equal footing with fellow pupils, and because verb tenses were explained and introduced in a structured way, she quickly assimilated them and was one of a few to use a range of tenses accurately. In English, she had learned from her peers and through reading, but she had not been taught verb use systematically. She went on to learn several European languages and embarked on an international career, where she was able to use Mandarin and Cantonese alongside a range of European languages. She was an example of an able pupil whose ability came to light through her performance in a foreign language, despite her – at the time – limited English.

Collaborative learning (group work)

This system allows for larger groups to be broken down into smaller ones to allow pupils to take on different roles in organising their own and others' learning. It is particularly suitable for MFL learning, where communication is the means and the end. Pupils can work on identical or complementary tasks and then share their output in a plenary. They could also develop their critical skills by assessing the performance of other groups, for example, in a drama or a PowerPoint presentation. Classes scheduled for the same timetable slot can be organised to work as one large group, 'performing' for each other. For example, a more able group could perform for a lower set, or a competition could be set up between two parallel classes.

At Key Stages 3 and 4, schools now have much more opportunity to develop flexible arrangements for their pupils than they had previously. They can therefore accommodate the learning needs of particularly able groups and individuals in imaginative and exciting ways. It is easier to find out and share ideas about special situations and therefore schools, parents and able pupils should be on the lookout for good opportunities.

Content and Language Integrated Learning (CLIL) – a model for the future?

CLIL covers any activity involving using a foreign language to learn a non-language subject. For years, many schools in Canada have been offering bilingual programmes from primary – and even kindergarten – level and throughout high schools. Within these programmes, certain subjects (maths or humanities subjects, for example) are taught in French, or in another language. In England, a project involving CILT and the University of Nottingham is in progress. One aspect under examination is how to award accreditation in both language (currently French or German) and non-language subjects (such as geography or history). Thus CLIL is a further model – albeit an ambitious one – that could prove inspiring to more able pupils. See the CILT website (www.cilt.org.uk) for case studies and future plans.

Allocation of resources

More able pupils are entitled to their fair share of all resources, staff time, time with any foreign language assistants, support time and materials, if their needs are to be met. Here is a suggestion from CILT:

> Departments should assemble a range of support and extension materials for both pupils and teachers. These should support extension and enrichment work across the four skills (listening, speaking, reading and writing), and, where possible, encourage integrated skill activities. It may be possible to set up a central access point within the department covering different languages, so that the material is available to different groups of pupils at different times.
>
> (www.qca.org.uk/qca_2277.aspx)

Mentors, parents, governors, members of staff in other departments and foreign language assistants may help to build up the resources collection. Items to include in the collection are:

- reference materials – printed and electronic

- dictionaries – monolingual and bilingual

- grammar reference books, at various levels of difficulty

- extended verb reference books/CDs

- self-study, extended reading and listening materials with, eventually, follow-up tasks, for example Authentik (www.authentik.com)

- literature, including poetry, drama, DVDs, videos

- computers –

  - to allow access via the internet to authentic language resources on a range of topics, for staff and pupils

- to enable e-mail links with pupils who speak the target language

- to publish pupils' work in the target language

- to allow pupils to prepare and give presentations.

Heads of department whose schools were within the EiC (Excellence in Cities) scheme had access to funding for projects for more able pupils. The school gifted and talented coordinator and LA adviser should be good sources of information for possible funding for special initiatives. Working within a consortium will also open up opportunities.

Liaison with other departments

The following are some issues/opportunities, involving communication with other departments, which can be exploited to the benefit of all:

- developing joint projects of a cross-curricular nature, for example, a geography field trip abroad or a visit to an art gallery to study their collection of French or Spanish paintings

- working with teachers of subjects who have skills and/or interests in MFL

- liaising over selection

- taking advantage of possibilities of overlap between curriculum areas, for talented pupils in particular, but also for able pupils with interests in art, music, the performing arts, and sport: for example, music students studying German (or French/Spanish/Italian/Japanese etc.) musicians; singing in other languages

- pupils with talent in sports, to learn about that sport using the target language (TL), or to study the career of well-known players who speak that language

- pupils with talent in dance/performing arts to study the career of dancers from another culture, read/write reviews in the target language(s), perform a piece based on a model from another culture

- language pupils acting as interpreters to allow their talented peers to access materials, writing, contacts in a given field (sport, music . . .) in other cultures; pupils acting as cultural attachés when the school is hosting/making a music/sports tour.

Example

One girls' school finds that music and dance are particularly popular with their 11–18 age group. Pupils contributed to a cultural evening upon return from a trip to Germany at the end of the summer term, performing to a high standard despite the many other demands they faced at this time of the year.

Monitoring and assessment

Monitoring and assessment go hand in hand with policy making. In monitoring the progress of the more able, their teacher and head of department will be looking for evidence that these pupils are moving up through the Key Stage 3 and GCSE levels and being given the opportunities to raise their achievement.

This can be done by lesson observation – to check that the more able are being given a chance to try out more challenging tasks, to judge whether the classroom atmosphere supports high achievement, to speak to pupils about their work and so on. It can be done by interviews with individual pupils and looking at what they have produced. This could take the form of a brief interview either in or out of class – or even a telephone call. It can also be done by looking at the teacher's lesson planning and discussing outcomes. Able pupils – as a rule – report that they really value the chance to talk to teachers about their work.

Technology can also help to track progress, particularly on those smaller components of language acquisition (for example, vocabulary) that need to keep growing, but are time-consuming to mark. The effects of the DfES circular 2/98 *Reducing the Bureaucratic Burden on Teachers* are producing innovative systems to deal with data which should lighten teachers' load. Computer programmes can test vocabulary, listening skills and pronunciation – and keep records of scores.

From Year 7, all pupils, not just the more able, should be encouraged to use what they know about extending their skills in English to upgrade their own performance in their MFL. More able pupils could use a grammar checklist to look at technical details (Do the subjects and verbs agree? Do the adjectives agree with nouns? Are the adjectives in the correct position?). They should also be encouraged to assess work by their peers and give feedback as this will in turn improve their own work.

In order for pupils to be able to self-assess, they need to be very clear about criteria. Displays linking 'user-friendly' translations of criteria, together with examples, should always be available for pupils to consult. They could be printed in pupils' learning diaries or organisers and/or pasted into exercise books or folders as well as displayed on the classroom wall.

Tasks modelled on the Key Stage 3 optional tests and tasks in MFL (first published by SCAA, QCA's predecessor) can be used as end-of-term or end-of-year assessments. (NB There are updated materials which can be downloaded from the QCA website and inserted into the original test booklets.)

There will be further discussion of recording and assessment in Chapter 4.

Individual education plans (IEPs)

One example of providing a simple and effective monitoring system for exceptional pupils is the individual education plan. IEPs are more common for pupils with special educational needs, but they are also suitable for those exceptional pupils whose needs do not fit within the school's grouping. The pupil is encouraged to reflect on his or her learning and to record successes. The pupil also meets on a regular basis with the head of department to discuss targets, to share feedback and to set new targets – which should not just be academic ones.

An example of an IEP is given below.

<u>*School Name*</u>

Able Pupil's Individual Education Plan for FRENCH

<u>**Autumn Term 200_**</u>

Name of Pupil: _____

Form/Year Group: _____

Summary of background evidence of higher ability in Modern Foreign Languages:

Targets set for this term:

    1) _____

    2) _____

    3) _____

Review Date: _____

(Spring Term 20--) Comments on progress made:

Signed (Pupil): _____

Signed (Teacher): _____

Signed (Parent/Carer): _____

Date: _____

Able Pupil's Individual Education Plan

INSET activities for the department

Activity 1: how to recognise a more able language learner

This could be part of the departmental 'articulation and discussion', considered so important by Ofsted, as part of the process of agreeing on and internalising the concept. The descriptions of a more able language learner are taken from the QCA website.

Pupils who are gifted in modern foreign languages are likely to:	What activities can the teacher organise in the classroom for these behaviours to be displayed and observed?
1. have a strong desire to put language together by themselves they apply principles from what they have learned to new situations, transforming phrases and using them in a different context, often with humour	Encourage experimentation.
2. show creativity and imagination when using language they often extend the boundaries of their knowledge and work beyond what they have learned, not wishing simply to respond and imitate, but to initiate exchanges and to create new language	Pupils can devise role-plays or a mini-play.
3. have a natural feel for languages they are willing to take risks and see what works, knowing instinctively what sounds right and what looks right; they are acutely and swiftly aware of the relationship between sound and spelling	Teacher can encourage pupils to find out about the difference between, say acute and grave accents and introduce pupils to the International Phonetic Alphabet.
4. pick up new language and structures quickly they may have excellent aural and oral skills and may be able to cope with rapid streams of sound and identify key words at an early stage; they may also display outstanding powers of retention, both immediately and from one lesson to the next	Teacher can set up a quick recall session at the beginning of lesson/unit.
5. make connections and classify words and structures to help them learn more efficiently they are able to evaluate new language critically, recognising the grammatical function of words	Teacher can ask pupils to group words by function and to justify their system/classifications.
6. seek solutions and ask further questions they may test out their theories and seek to solve linguistic problems, sometimes challenging the tasks set and trying to understand their relevance to the language-learning process	Give pupils opportunity to set their own tasks; set open-ended task with a time limit.
7. have an insight into their own learning style and preference they may say how they like to learn vocabulary or structures; they are clear about the type of tasks they like doing; they may show or display an ability to work independently, without supervision, and to make effective use of reference material	Get feedback during profiling (formative assessment) sessions. Provide a starter list of reference materials – display – give pupils opportunity to add to it.
8. show an intense interest in the cultural features of the language being studied they may use idiom in the language itself and explore the history and the traditions of the language; some pupils may wish to share their knowledge with their peers	Set optional homework or projects 'Where do languages come from?' 'Where does French/Urdu/Spanish/German come from?'

Characteristics of a more able language learner
Adapted from www.nc.uk.net/gt/languages/index.htm

Without looking at the right-hand column, staff can look at the descriptors (1–8) and think about, then share their ideas on:

- What conditions are conducive to these behaviours?

- How can these behaviours be detected in the classroom – or out of it?

- How can the department support any pupils who might be reluctant to reveal these abilities?

- How can the department share this information with pupils so that they can also realise they are gifted?

Some suggestions are given in the right-hand column.

Activity 2, part one: countering misconceptions about high ability

This could be a further step in ongoing departmental discussion. It is sometimes useful to challenge teachers' assumptions, such as with this exercise, suggested by George (1997: 32–33) and based on a list devised by Richard Lange and Mark German.

1. Read through the following lists and check which items are misconceptions.

2. Tick which three you agree with the most and star those you disagree with and consider to be myths.

3. Think of the most gifted and talented child you know and circle which items apply to that particular individual.

4. Discuss your conclusions with your colleagues.

Myths and misconceptions

'Gifted children':
- have everything going their way
- are more emotionally stable and mature than their non-gifted peers
- prefer to work alone
- are model students
- always reveal their giftedness
- are organised and neat
- are well rounded
- are creative
- are good learners
- are very verbal
- have good handwriting

- are good spellers
- have very supportive parents and come from good homes
- have a low tolerance for slower students
- are perfectionists
- work harder than average kids
- look or act differently.

Activity 2, part two: profile of an underachiever

Read the profile of an underachiever (George 1997: 12). Do you recognise any of your pupils in these descriptions?

Profile of an underachiever

- poor test performance
- orally knowledgeable but poor in written work
- superior comprehension and retention of concepts when interested
- apparently bored
- achieving below expectations in basic subjects
- restless or inattentive
- daily work often incomplete or poorly done
- dislikes practice work
- tactless and impatient of slower minds
- prefers friendship with older pupils or adults
- excessively self-critical
- unable to make good relationships with peer group and teachers
- emotionally unstable – low self-esteem, withdrawn and sometimes aggressive
- has wide range of interests and possibly an area of real expertise.

Activity 3: building language-learning skills and giving feedback

This activity is intended to allow staff to consider a sample of writing from the National Curriculum website and then to focus on some of the principles of assessment for learning. The following materials are required:

- writing by Year 9 pupil '*Mon collège*' (Neil Clark) – available from www.ncaction.org.uk/search/comment.htm?id=2160
- commentary samples on this piece of writing (given below)
- level descriptors for attainment target 4: Writing – available from www.ncaction.org.uk/subjects/mfl/levels.htm

- poster: Research-based principles of assessment for learning to guide classroom practice – available from www.qca.org.uk/libraryassets/media/ 4031_afl_principles.pdf

Commentary on text

Activity description

This activity was part of the end-of-year assessment for this fast track top set. The pupils had done preparatory work on schools in class, and the teacher asked them to produce an extended piece of written work advertising their school to others.

Activity Objectives

To assess pupils' writing in examination conditions.

Commentary

Neil has used a range of tenses accurately and has given a lot of information about his school. His writing is sometimes repetitive and, when he has tried to be more ambitious, inaccurate. This is characteristic of Level 6 in writing. However, in the length, structure and register of his writing, Neil is starting to demonstrate characteristics of Level 7.

- Staff read '*Mon collège*' and note evidence of competence (for example, tenses) as well as errors.

- Staff read level descriptors, try to agree on a level, then look at the commentary provided.

- Staff consider the question: How can Neil extend his language skills? Firstly, it might be useful to consider accuracy: difference between *an/année*; *chaque* cannot be used with a plural noun, by definition; use of the partitive; noun/verb agreement. Secondly, consider how to build complexity into some sentences: Neil can practise with models of *si* clauses and of clauses with *qui, ce que*. Thirdly, looking ahead to Level 8, ask Neil a) to consider whether he has answered the question set (the teacher asked them 'to produce an extended piece of written work advertising their school to others') and b) whether he and his 'work buddy' can think of ways of redrafting the piece using some questions.

- Staff read the poster: Research-based principles of assessment for learning to guide classroom practice. The importance of this representation is that it is research-based, not just another 'to do' list handed down from above. Number these principles 1–10 left to right to ease discussion in the next step.

- Taking these principles into consideration one by one, how would staff go about giving Neil (and/or his class) feedback on his writing? Here are some suggestions:

  - **Point one (planning)**. Go over grammar points common to all pupils; take pupils' suggestions on points they would like covered.

- **Point two (how students learn)**. Get pupils to report (in their planners, in pairs etc.) on how they went about composing and then memorising the piece. They could all contribute to a list of 'good advice' on strategies – to pass on to next year's Year 9 pupils.

- **Points three, four and ten are reasons for doing this INSET task!** But it's an opportunity for teachers and pupils to reflect on the point that 'reading' an assessment is a skilled and time-consuming job; that both teacher and pupil are being tested and want to get good results, and that pupils too can improve their assessing skills with practice. It is about building confidence.

- **Point five (sensitive and constructive)**. Make time for one-to-one discussion; ask Neil how he feels about his work. Does he see how his increased grammatical mastery can be extended to other topics?

- **Point six (foster motivation)**. Get Neil to compare his work with earlier writing – and highlight signs of his progress. In particular, in Year 9, he has made a good start on using the perfect tense – probably the most difficult technical step for young anglophone learners of French to take. He has also used the imperfect appropriately and accurately. Many francophone pupils do not write as accurately as this! If he were writing in English, how would he liven this piece up to make it more like advertising copy? There is nothing in the brief about the account being honest, so he is free to use his imagination and sense of humour. He could make some exciting claims about (future) plans to develop the school: offering gourmet breakfasts in the canteen for those who arrive early. He could say what he would prefer to wear (using the conditional) as a uniform and think up some good reasons why.

- **Point seven (understanding of goals and criteria)**. Get Neil and his classmates to look at each other's work, link phrases in the descriptors at Levels 6, 7 and 8 with examples – or gaps – in their writing; consider the difference between 'express' ideas and 'express and justify'? Do they know what reference materials they could use and how to use them? For example, if they need reminding about using *de*, where can they look it up and can they make sense of the explanations and examples. If not, why not?

- **Point eight (give constructive guidance, opportunity to improve, eliminate weaknesses)**. Neil has done well with adjective agreements so he should be encouraged to keep using adjectives in his descriptions and build up his repertoire of adjectives, preferably with adverbs attached 'amazingly interesting', 'unbelievably fascinating'. For examples he could look through some online advertisements for, say, sports equipment. To work on eliminating errors, the teacher could collect a list of 'top 10 no-nos', display them and keep referring to them until they have been eliminated: for example *DE + LE, BEACOUP*! They could all check their partner's work before each piece of writing is handed in, making a game of it or putting it on the wall as a class target; they could be allowed to pick a favourite activity or have a prize if they manage to hand in a complete set of work without these errors . . .

- **Point nine**. Ask the class to look back and find an example of where they have self-assessed – corrected a spelling mistake, for example. How did they recognise it as a mistake?

Activity 3

Consider the unit voted 'most boring' by the most able pupils during Year 8. What reasons did the pupils give? What can be done to launch the topic more successfully next time, make it more fun but challenging at the same time?

Summary

- The head of department has certain obligations towards the most able pupils in MFL.
- The head of department must be clear about what is meant by effective provision for more able pupils – and be committed to ensuring it.
- An audit is an effective tool for answering the questions – Where are we now? Where is there good practice? Where are changes needed?
- The department can produce a good working policy document by clarifying and pooling ideas.
- The most able pupils are entitled to their fair share of appropriate resources; a variety of resources are being developed and made available.
- Liaising with other departments can spark creative projects and spread resources.
- Meetings and training days are good opportunities for teachers to use each other as a resource and there are many group activities that can stimulate thought.
- Good quality systems for monitoring and evaluation will help answer the question 'Where have we succeeded and what do we need to focus on next?'

CHAPTER 3

Recognising high ability and potential

- What are the characteristics of the most able MFL pupils?
- Learning styles, multiple intelligences and collaborative learning
- Creativity and 'task commitment'

Schools become more effective in identifying able children as they get better at providing for them.

(Eyre 1997: 25)

The purpose of this chapter is to consider the salient qualities of very able MFL pupils, so that such pupils can be recognised as early as possible in the classroom and given the opportunities they need to fulfil their potential.

What are the characteristics of the most able MFL pupils?

It is often harder to judge pupils' true abilities in MFL than in other curriculum areas. Since second-language learners in England usually begin in a school setting, learners – even the most gifted – have already passed the critical period at which their language acquisition skills are at their best. Pupil learners are much more dependent on the skill of their teachers than in other subjects. Some aspects of linguistic ability depend on the individual's development and may therefore not come into play until late in their secondary school career. For these reasons, teachers need to keep an open mind and to look out for opportunities for pupils to go beyond basic tasks and achieve at a higher level.

There does seem to be such a thing as language-learning aptitude, but it eludes definition. Research on the 'good language learner' (GLL) has revealed certain important factors:

- general 'intelligence'

- aptitude: grammatical, discourse, sociolinguistic competence, memory, aural assimilation and discrimination, rapid learning

- personality: e.g. risk-taking, lack of inhibition

- age of acquisition: 'critical period hypothesis' is well supported by research (including current brain research)

- motivation and attitude: positive attitudes and intrinsic and instrumental motivation (perhaps advantaging older learners)

- learner preferences/styles

- learner beliefs: e.g. in the value of language learning and in their ability to succeed

and

- learner strategies: the GLL appears to be conscious of what works best for them and consciously applies successful strategies (cognitive, metacognitive and social).

(adapted from Lightbown and Spada 1993, quoted by Eyre and Lowe 2002: 142)

Many of these factors could be inferred from a range of information about pupils even before they began a MFL.

QCA provides a description of how pupils gifted in MFL are likely to behave. It is useful as a basis for discussion, especially to do with provision, but less useful as a checklist. It describes behaviours which would show when an able pupil was well on the way, not in the very early stages. Not all able learners will show all these behaviours: some will be much more skilled in certain aspects of language learning than in others. Furthermore, there is an intimate relationship between these behaviours and the opportunity to display them. In some very able pupils, these characteristics will not be revealed in Year 7, or even Year 11 – even if suitable opportunities are given – but will come out when the learner is more mature or becomes highly motivated.

Checklists can be problematic as they tend to make the process of identifying the more able pupil appear to be a simple one. This is far from the reality.

As regards departmental criteria, it may be helpful to use examples [of checklists] for discussion, but a simple incorporation of someone else's approach into the departmental handbook will not be effective. It is the thinking, the reflecting and the consideration of the implications for teaching which are crucial to the success of the exercise.

(Eyre 1997: 19)

It is really for the department, therefore, to come up with its own checklist, as an INSET exercise. Here are some suggestions of pupil behaviours, skills or attitudes to watch for:

- asking questions or volunteering information about related words in English or their first language

- making links

- being curious and perceptive about cultural differences

- accurately replicating new vocabulary or expressions

- remembering what they heard; discriminating aurally between similar sounds

- imitating intonation, gestures, inflection, stress patterns accurately

- picking up details (in writing, for example, using accents accurately)

- imitating written patterns accurately

- spotting how a sentence 'works'

- using a dictionary effectively

- grasping grammar points (for example, verb inflection system, adjective agreement) quickly and accurately

- preferring to use technical vocabulary to discuss language

- knowing and applying grammatical terms

- making many/interesting variations on a model sentence

- enjoying playing with language, being creative (for example, inventing 'silly' versions of conversations, inventing inappropriate replies)

- asking 'Why?' questions

- asking questions about structures

- having a rich vocabulary, good reading skills and good comprehension in their first language

- having a good memory.

Although any one pupil would not exhibit all these behaviours or characteristics, they will all be recognisable and appreciated by a MFL teacher. Because it is so problematic to judge potential in MFL, the department needs to cast a wide net to gather information. Other means of identifying potential, a combination of the qualitative and the quantitative, and based on a Year 7 cohort are listed below.

Analysing 'objective' test results

National Curriculum Key Stage 2 tests (the pupil's average point score); Cognitive Ability Tests (CATs); MidYis tests; reading test scores; sub-scores, especially Verbal Reasoning results – all these measures may provide useful clues. Bear in mind that there is no such thing as a perfect test, that an able child may produce a low score for various reasons, for example, using another language outside school or having attention deficit disorder (ADD). The school may also consider other ways of assessing general ability if it has a significant cohort of EAL (English as an Additional Language) pupils.

It is up to the MFL department to decide how to use this information. Some will decide to group at the beginning of Year 7 on the basis of this information, and then to review the situation throughout the year.

Sharing input from feeder schools

Scanning primary school reports can give a picture of the whole child, revealing potential and/or underachievement. Some MFL staff will prefer to form their own impressions of pupils in their Year 7 groups first, and refer to primary reports after a few weeks.

Close links with feeder schools will help to evaluate the evaluators at primary level. As happens in the secondary school, a 'gifted' child in one population may not be considered as such in another.

As part of the National Languages Strategy, MFL will be a statutory requirement in the primary curriculum in Key Stage 2. Before September 2009, therefore, there will have to be a considerable amount of cross-phase planning. As part of this ambitious project, schools may opt to use the European Languages Portfolio to record and communicate children's experiences and progress in languages other than English.

Using departmental judgement, observation and discussion

The professional judgement of the MFL teacher, when that teacher has a clear idea of what to look for, will outweigh more official-looking test results. But 'a teacher's subjective assessment of a pupil can be inaccurate if the teacher tends to rate most highly those pupils who are persevering, conforming, tidy and industrious' (George 1997: 29–30). Thus it is essential that the department has a shared view, an ongoing discussion and that individual teachers are alert to the needs of the pupil who is ready for challenging work.

Pupils may have developed considerably during the summer – they may even have spent part of the summer in a French/Spanish/German environment. Pupils are often highly motivated if they are taking up this 'new' subject in Year 7.

As staff have a chance to assess and observe pupils for themselves, some departments will decide to divide the Year 7 group into sets at some point in the year: for example, at the beginning of term two, after February half-term or at the beginning of term 3.

Considering information from outside the department

Some pupils will have been identified as more able in English, maths, science, etc. These pupils have already demonstrated potential and/or motivation. It is likely that MFL teachers will benefit more than most from the observations of colleagues in other subjects. This is to be expected, not just because pupils are in the early stages of 'foreign' language learning. A pupil judged to be more able in English is likely to have high potential in MFL.

Some pupils will have been identified as 'talented' in other areas: PE, music, dance, art, drama, technology (including information technology). A dance or music teacher, for example, may have noticed a pupil with an outstanding memory.

Having another look – as part of ongoing assessment and monitoring

Liaise with the SEN department, in case a pupil's special needs are interfering with their MFL learning. Note whether there any under-represented groups. Try to identify possible underachievers. It is worth noting that 18% of pupils in a correctional centre were identified as more able! Ask: 'Could there be hidden talents here?'

Consulting pupils

During formative reporting sessions, ask pupils to say who are the best linguists in their group and to give their reasons. Allow pupils to nominate themselves, but bear in mind that able children may have no measure of what is average. They may be able to memorise 100 items of vocabulary in a few minutes and assume everyone can do the same! Also, look for 'task-commitment' (see the comments on the Renzulli rings, below). A genuine love of languages should be given more weight than 'objective' test results. Ask pupils about other language learning experience, including home languages or family expertise.

When the MFL department's 'more able' cohort has been agreed upon, circulate it to all language teachers. Use a code to indicate pupils in registers/mark books so that teachers and supply staff cannot overlook them.

Departments need to make provisional lists for each year group and keep them continually under review to ensure that pupils with potential to excel at languages are not missed. Departments should also devise their own checklists and refine them as their expertise develops.

Learning styles, multiple intelligences and collaborative learning

Before we look at providing for able pupils in MFL, we need to look at some current ideas on ability and intelligence. Recent research attempts to map the brain have given a picture of each learner as having a unique pattern of strengths and weaknesses, although different researchers use different labels. Such theory leads to the necessity for teacher and learner to know about that unique picture, in order to develop potential.

Another influential strand of research on learning as a social activity (Vygotsky: 1978) has revealed how children can learn from each other and achieve more together than they would have done separately. Timely intervention (by a child or an adult) can be highly stimulating and productive. When we hear it said that society needs people who are able to work in groups to respond to complex problems, to provide imaginative ways through a set of challenges in an ever-changing world, we realise that the collaborative learning model is relevant not just to education.

The theory: learning styles and how they develop

Many researchers have tried to measure ability, using research tools which they have designed, without being aware that their findings would be a function of the tool they had chosen. An example would be the early versions of IQ tests (such as the Stanford-Binet Intelligence Scales), which measured what was later described as verbal reasoning. With more evolved technology, researchers can look at and attempt to map the brain and its activities in new ways, but are far from having definitive answers. At this point, we can say that our brains are specialised and that the left half of the brain uses words to express thoughts, while the right side 'thinks', but not in words. Researchers also agree that, just as with other organs of the body, one side of our brain is dominant. This concept would explain how we as different learners develop 'preferences' for particular learning styles.

These theories, as with their predecessors, are landmarks on the way to mapping the brain: imperfect landmarks, but perhaps the best we have at the moment. Most teachers are dependent on educational and other researchers to articulate and publicise their findings, although talented, intuitive teachers often reach similar conclusions. Therefore, as we seek to identify the gifted language learner, it makes sense to use a combination of tools, such as research-based checklists, plus the input of the professional (teacher), the parent/carer (who has observed their child over time) and the child/learner.

Teachers, who – on the whole – have been successful learners in their own subjects, tend to favour styles which have worked for them. In recent years, and particularly in England, teachers and pupils have been encouraged to find ways of using and responding to a range of teaching and learning styles. Attention has also focused on the educational value of looking at the learning process itself. Teachers and learners have been encouraged to share their intended aims and outcomes. Pupils have been encouraged to think about how they learn, their strengths and weaknesses, and to set targets for themselves.

Using knowledge about learning styles and learning preferences

There is a lack of consistency over use of these terms. Richard Riding (2002: 22) makes a helpful distinction between

- cognitive style – 'an individual's preferred and habitual approach to organising and representing information'

- learning preferences – the individual's preferences for structure, presentation, type of content that suits their cognitive style, and

- learning strategies – what is developed by the learner to adapt the task to their preferred style.

If a school has decided that it is desirable for all teachers and pupils to be aware of their teaching and learning preference/styles, it may be carrying out work with pupils on a whole-school basis, perhaps within PSHE lessons, and then sharing the results via pupils' organisers or learning diaries. Within a MFL lesson, pupils could carry out a similar survey in the target language. A simple questionnaire (in English, which could be translated by either pupils or teachers) for use within the department is available at www.english.qmul.ac.uk/ShakesinClass/LearningPrefsQuest.html.

When we come to planning, we need to bear in mind that it is good for pupils to be able to take in and process information in a variety of ways, and not to be limited to their preferred style alone. They will not always be given the choice in the world outside school.

For the very able, and particularly those very able language learners with special educational needs, it may be worth their time to consider whether they are 'verbalisers' (thinking in words) or 'imagers' (thinking in pictures); 'wholists' (seeing the big picture rather than the parts) or 'analytics' (seeing the parts rather than the whole picture). Learners cannot change their cognitive styles but they – and their teachers – can develop learning strategies to help them deal with a mismatch between their own style and the way the material is presented. A good example would be using headings and sub-headings as signposts in presentations (written or oral or a combination of the two) to help the 'wholist' impose a structure on the information that is being transmitted.

These ideas will come into play when we consider case studies in Chapter 5, since there is some evidence of strong links between certain styles and problem classroom behaviours (Riding 2002: 63).

The theory of multiple intelligences

The author's first acquaintance with the idea of multiple intelligences came at an Association for Language Learning (ALL) conference workshop. After an exposition, a group of modern languages teachers were set the challenge of devising tasks to exploit pupils' different 'intelligences'. This was an attempt to put into practice the theory of 'the world according to Gardner', based on Howard Gardner's *Frames of Mind: The Theory of Multiple Intelligences* (1983/2003), and

1	Verbal–linguistic	good with words
2.	Logical–mathematical	good with numbers and puzzles
3.	Visual–spatial	good with pictures
4.	Bodily–kinaesthetic	'body smart', for example, quickly picking up and remembering dance moves, instinctively taking up the most effective position or move while playing sport
5.	Musical	very responsive to rhythm and music in general
6.	Interpersonal	good with other people and in teams
7.	Intrapersonal	good self-knowledge, reflective, with insight into one's own emotions
8.	Naturalistic	observant and aware of the natural world, good at classifying

Eight possible intelligences (after Howard Gardner)

was an entertaining and educational experience. It certainly revealed many non-linguistic talents among the teachers.

Above is a description of the eight possible intelligences identified by Gardner. It is useful to be aware of these categories, even though not all of them have a high correlation with the abilities usually associated with a more able language learner. But knowing something about them can provide a 'way in' to languages for a particular learner. As part of a professional development session, the teacher can ask 'How can these intelligences be used to promote the pupil's language learning?' For pupils, insight into the possible ranges of intelligences and learning styles, their own and others' preferences and talents, is a valuable part of their lifelong learning project.

The Key Stage 3 (KS3) National Strategy document shows how these intelligences relate to writing.

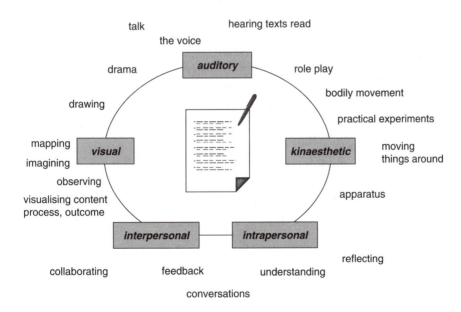

Learning styles and writing in modern foreign languages
Taken from *KS3 National Strategy – Learning Styles and Writing in MFL*, DfES 0382/2002

Intelligence	Pupils may be able to use the MFL to . . .
Verbal–linguistic	Write advertising copy to promote the city/region as a venue for the Olympics.
Logical–mathematical	Choose a French (German, Spanish, Italian . . .) town or village and discuss comparative statistics, showing similarities and differences between it and 'home'. Use French (Spanish, etc.) websites to research the statistics.
Visual–spatial	Sketch and label suitable visual material (such as a coloured pictorial map), using colours, and shapes for a mural or a brochure to convey accurately a sense of their town/region.
Bodily–kinaesthetic	Explain with words and diagrams why their town's football team is successful/unsuccessful this season.
Musical	Choose a piece of music that is typical of their region. How would they explain their choice to a French (etc.) speaker? Or, compose a rap using the advertising copy written to promote the city as a venue for the Olympics.
Interpersonal	Work with their group to invent a series of interviews with townspeople representing different viewpoints: young people, families, old-timers, recent immigrants.
Intrapersonal	Write an account of what it is like to grow up in their home town.
Naturalistic	Draw up a list of wildlife or plants typical of the area. Consider and write about recommended places to walk a dog. Produce and label some photographs of local gardens or allotments and the plants they contain.

Using multiple intelligences in the languages classroom – an example

The above table gives some suggestions of ways pupils could examine the topic *'Ma ville/mon village'* to exploit their individual intelligences – their strengths.

Creativity and 'task commitment'

One of the major errors that continues to be made in identifying potential in the more able is to ignore two other areas, or 'clusters' of traits which – according to the findings of Renzulli (1977) – are as important as high ability. High scores in IQ-type tests are not reliable predictors of school performance. This is because 'task-commitment' and 'creativity' are equally important. Where the three clusters interact, truly gifted behaviour will occur.

The picture of the 'good language learner' mentioned above is consistent with the idea of 'task commitment' (which includes motivation, persistence, resilience, love of the subject) – the 'ideal pupil'? The MFL teacher should also be on the lookout for the pupil with novel ideas and approaches – perhaps easiest to spot when expressed as humour and quirkiness.

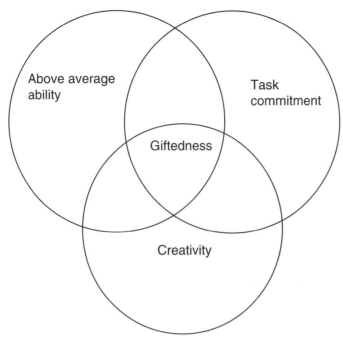

The Renzulli Rings, or what makes giftedness

The work of Vygotsky

Vygotsky's research confronted one of the key practices in IQ testing: the child was required to solve problems on their own. It was assumed that the level reached was reliably the highest possible. Vygotsky's observations led him to argue that intelligence has a social origin. The same child often had the capacity to perform at a higher level with the benefit of help, whether from a peer, caregiver or teacher. Another child, with the same help, could not. From these observations and further research by many educators has grown a teaching and learning model with a set of key concepts:

- the 'zone of proximal development' – the name Vygotsky gave to the difference between what the learner achieves alone and the achievement with input from someone else. In other words, the zone where learning can take place.

- scaffolding – the support the learner uses to reach a higher level. When s/he can do without scaffolding, s/he is said to be able to do the task, or set of tasks, independently.

- collaborative learning – learning as a social activity.

- effective communication (talk) about the problem and how to solve it.

- the teacher – as mediator, who:

  - facilitates

  - establishes rules/conventions, for example 'argue against the ideas, not the person'

- structures groups

- can assign roles within the group, for example, a spokesperson, timekeeper

- models

- demonstrates or shows her/his own thinking process 'thinking aloud' as s/he works through a problem

- coaches

- gives clues, feedback.

- context – the closer a task is to a real-world situation, the better.

- linking the problem to what the learner already knows.

This model underlines the key point that learning occurs as a result of an opportunity, plus a 'boost' that moves the learner on and gives the teacher a sense of the pupil's potential.

Various classroom-based studies in several countries have also been influenced by the research of Vygotsky but have specifically centred on teaching reading. The development of the Literacy Strategy in primary schools in England (now extended into secondary schools) has grown from these studies. Those concerned with the language development of young people have recognised the power of 'modelling' reading, writing and speaking interactions, as ways of providing 'scaffolding' to support and give direction to pupils' linguistic growth. The underlying interest in the language of texts is reflected in the way the Key Stage 3 National Strategy and MFL framework is set out: texts are still texts, even if they are in a modern foreign language.

A related point here is one made earlier: a pupil with excellent skills in their first language – who has shown considerable reading capability – should be considered as a good candidate for the 'more able' cohort in a MFL. There will still be pupils whose potential is revealing itself more slowly, however – who are waiting to be discovered!

Summary

- Identifying very able modern linguists is a complex task.

- Departments need to gather information from many sources, to discuss their criteria and their pupils.

- Departments should keep their lists under review as pupils move through the school. They should also devise their own identification checklists and refine them as their expertise develops.

- Teachers and pupils need to be aware of how they learn, so that they can be more effective in their roles.

CHAPTER 4

Classroom provision

- Planning – the theory
- Enrichment – the concept
- Differentiation – the concept
- Differentiation – the practice
- Lesson beginnings and endings
- Skills needed by the most able and ways of developing them
- Higher order skills
- Asking questions
- Homework
- Recording and assessment for multiple intelligences
- Endnote

Teaching is a highly skilled and demanding activity, and in recent years teachers have been hard-pressed by the many changes and developments they have been required to introduce to their classrooms. Nevertheless, with care and imagination, appropriate and relevant learning opportunities can be planned for the great majority of children with exceptional abilities within the context of their regular classrooms.

(Leyden 1998: 58)

This chapter will map out how teachers can plan for the delivery of challenging lessons, tasks, and follow-up to its more able pupils. The starting point will depend on the individual school and its policies and on the individual department within the school. From there, the department needs to ask, 'What are we looking for in a challenging lesson and how can we be sure to recognise it when we see it?'

Planning – the theory

Here is a good description of what the teacher is attempting to do when planning for the more able, suggested by Clark and Callow (2002: 94–5):

Find lesson structures, materials and methodologies that encourage the pupils to:

- speculate and generate ideas with imagination and originality
- expand their knowledge base and stretch their memories; question perceptively and demand logical responses from others
- challenge accepted ideas and arguments
- work independently, searching with confidence for meaning and pattern in abstract and concrete tasks
- present ideas clearly and logically
- gain experience in interpolation and extrapolation, deducing outcomes and making inferences.

Expect pupils to:

- work at a fast pace, assimilating and processing data rapidly and leaping stages in arguments and processes
- handle multiple variables and adapt to new ideas and situations rapidly
- make clear, precise, apposite responses to questions or tasks
- produce work that is well presented, grammatical, accurate, rigorous
- achieve an effective balance between selectivity and detail
- evaluate their own work objectively and the work of others constructively
- work cooperatively, accept valid criticism and respect the views of others.

How can these principles be turned into practice by the department? Bearing these points in mind may help:

- Such change is not easy to effect, but . . .
- teachers are good learners. If they compare their experience they can build on it together. The process of thinking through, working collaboratively, is key.
- It is better to focus on only one area at a time.
- The reward is that reframing the teaching and learning process to improve its effectiveness for the more able should bring out good teaching and learning in general – and thus raise achievement for all pupils.

INSET activity

Beginning with a section or topic from the existing scheme of work, think about its effectiveness for the more able, referring to the above principles, for example:

Does it encourage imaginative and original responses? Does it encourage independent work? Reflect on how well the section/topic has led to good responses from pupils in the past. A bank of such responses – a portfolio of outstanding work – can serve as models for future pupils. It can also be used for open evenings, records of achievement, exemplars for assessment.

Three planning models which can help to add challenge

Use of these models is based on the idea that able pupils will be, for most of their lessons, in classrooms in comprehensive schools. However, even in selective schools, differentiation for the most able will still be necessary and these models can still be used. The idea is to provide challenge for these pupils and to make it clear how they can branch out from the 'basic' programme (what is provided for others in their year group), to move to higher levels of competence and complexity. Examples of three models are given.

Must, should, could

This is a clear system that shows what activities might be offered in a given topic to take account of different levels of ability in a group. The core *must* be done by all pupils; those who master it *should* move on to the next task; only those who successfully complete the work at the second level move on to the *could* section. This is the model used in the Schemes of Work on the Standards Site: www.standards.dfes.gov.uk. An extract from the scheme of work for Year 8 French is given on the next page.

Note that we are not aiming at keeping pupils racing through one activity after another. Pupils may be ready to leap to the next stage in a progression (they may have grasped a complex point about language structure while others will need much more prompting, practice and reinforcement), but they will also benefit from time to process and reflect upon what they have learned and how to exploit and develop it. An individual or group may need to spend quite some time on a topic in order to explore it to their satisfaction. Nor is it a good idea to have our most able pupils producing a greater quantity of work than other pupils. If they can cover the *must* or even the *should* easily, they can move directly to the *could*, where the tasks require work of a different quality. The teacher needs to think ahead: how will s/he ascertain that some pupils are ready to move on? A quick question-answer session may be enough.

See Appendix 4.1 for a worked example of a way through the Year 8 Unit 11 topic *A la mode* from the Standards Site and see Appendix 4.2 for an example of one lesson within this sequence: demonstrative adjectives. In this example, the learning objectives for the lesson/unit of work (i.e. what the teacher intends the pupils to learn) are the same for the whole class, but the learning outcomes (what the pupils do to show what they have learned) will differ within the class.

Core/extension

This is a two-tier system similar to the above. Again, the core is the knowledge base that must be acquired for progression to occur. For the more

About the unit

In this unit pupils describe clothes and give their opinions about clothes. They learn how to use 'this' and 'these' with nouns and extend their knowledge of the perfect tense.

New language content:
- demonstrative adjectives
- comparisons
- more early steps with the perfect tense

New contexts:
- clothes and fashion
- styles and materials
- reading about clothes and fashion for information and pleasure

Alternative contexts: leisure activities; comparing, stating preferences; buying clothes; describing places and buildings (style, materials, changing fashions); describing pictures, photographs, works of art; food and drink.

This unit is expected to take 12–15 hours.

Where the unit fits in

This unit offers further opportunities for stating preferences. The initial use of the perfect tense is given more scope.

The learning of comparisons builds on the ability to describe things learnt in previous units.

Expectations

At the end of this unit

most pupils will: read and understand descriptions of clothes and fashions from a range of written and spoken sources; describe people and clothes in some detail, and state preferences, giving reasons; compare items of clothing, giving reasons for their suitability for different occasions; use the perfect tense to say what they wore on different occasions, without reliance on notes

some pupils will not have made so much progress and will: understand simple descriptions of clothes and fashions, including comparisons; ask for items of clothing, give simple descriptions and state preferences, using a model or other support; show some knowledge of the difference between present and perfect tenses

some pupils will have progressed further and will: describe clothes and fashions at length and in some detail, using a wide range of vocabulary; cope with some unfamiliar language in spoken or written material, and occasionally improvise

Extract from QCA scheme for Year 8 French: Unit 11 *A la mode*
www.standards.dfes.gov.uk/schemes2/secondary_mff/mff11/

able, it must be motivating and provide a kick-start into the block of work to be tackled.

The more able should move briskly through the core and on to the extension work, where they will have time for reflection and be able to try out new ideas. Extension activities must be qualitatively different, not just more of the same, and give pupils the opportunity to develop:

- independence

- critical thinking

- creative thinking

- problem-solving ability

- reflection

- motivation

- self-knowledge.

According to Deborah Eyre:

> In practice the creation of extension activities is not easy, especially at the start. It is not only about content or what is to be taught, but also about approaches to learning and thinking . . . These types of changes take time and, rather than adding extension to all lessons at once, it is advisable to choose one area for development so that targets can be set and progress monitored. In a secondary school this may be a selected year group which becomes the focus of departmental activity.
>
> (Eyre 1997: 54)

Example

In Unit 17 of MFL Key Stage 3 (French, but the activity is also suitable for use in Spanish and Italian), one of the learning objectives is use of relative pronouns (*qui/que*) to join two simple sentences, creating a subordinate clause. Pupils who have understood the principle of forming subordinate clauses in English may be able to move quickly to a stage where they can create their own in another language, while classmates need further practice and explanation.

An extension activity could be to create descriptions (of people, things, countries) for a class trivia quiz to be used later.

Another could be to see who could produce the longest sentence using a series of subordinate clauses.

As an excellent example of creative use of language, despite limited competence, the teacher could show a clip from a performance by comedian Eddie Izzard (available on CD). Having learned one French phrase: '*mon singe est dans l'arbre*', he manages to introduce it into many situations, using '*mon singe, qui est dans l'arbre*'. Pupils could use this as a model to be creative with relative pronouns and subordinate clauses.

Mind mapping

This is a useful planning tool to generate what the objectives of the lesson will be, before considering how the pupils will learn and how the teacher will know whether they have learned what was intended.

1. Use a whole page. Write the topic in the centre, in a centre circle or box.

2. Draw branches out to show sub-topics. If the sub-topics can also be divided, indicate this using further branches. Unless this is already highly readable (unlikely), do a tidier version, putting linked content together.

3. Once the content is clear, you can move on to how pupils are going to learn it and how to monitor and assess what is learned.

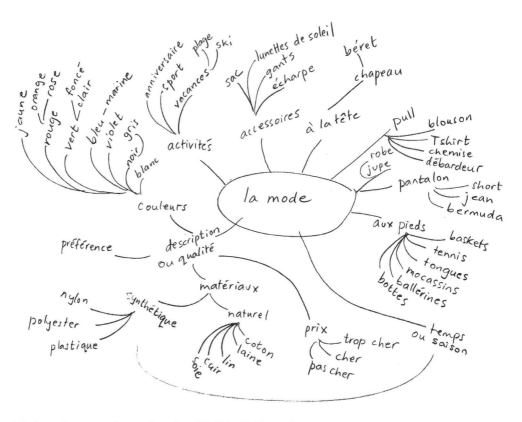

Mind map/planning diagram based on KS3 Unit 11 A la mode

Mind mapping is also a very useful device for students to use when planning or revising. In Appendix 4.1, there is an example of a lesson plan based on the idea of getting the pupils to produce a mind map to chart their own way through a topic.

Enrichment – the concept

What is enrichment? According to the Oxford Research Project (1985), quoted in George (1997: 99), it

- is a broadening and deepening of the learning experience

- provides experiences and activities beyond the regular curriculum

- develops the intellectual gifts and talents of the most able

- stresses qualitative development of thinking skills rather than quantitative accumulation of facts

- emphasises the process of learning rather than content

- can be horizontal, exploring bodies of knowledge that are not frequently touched upon in the school common core curriculum

- can be vertical, developing the skill of quantitative thinking which implies a facility with subject matter and ability to understand basic principles and to make generalisations

- generally involves children doing less and learning more. For example, it is usually preferable for a pupil to find three possible solutions to a problem than to solve three problems of a similar nature.

Enrichment, then, is a widely used term which is hard to define but seems to describe a process whereby the quality of the classroom experience moves beyond what is offered to the pupil in a given age group as core work.

> [Enrichment] is not about perfunctory completion of routine tasks, but about enlarging horizons, tackling problems whose solutions give rise to further problems, seeking peaks, experimenting with new materials, processes and ideas. It is also about enhancing the quality of life in the classroom and heightening sensitivity.
>
> (Eyre and Marjoram 1990 quoted in George 1997: 100–101)

The concept of enrichment goes hand in hand with that of differentiation. If 'differentiation is the process of matching learning experiences to individual needs' (George 1997: 105), then enrichment is the principal means of providing for the needs of the more able, although other pupils will also benefit. Examples of enrichment activities, which could be carried out either in the classroom, in lunchtime or after-school clubs, evening or weekend clubs, masterclasses, visits, or a summer school:

- a grammar quiz; a trivia quiz in a MFL

- a taster course in Asian languages or sign language

- (Cambridge) Latin online (www.cambridgescp.com)

- exploring the Greek alphabet and language; exploring linguistics or the International Phonetic Alphabet

- a once-a-month DVD club; movies in German, Spanish, Italian, French, various Asian languages

- dancing clubs: Bhangra music; salsa

- international or cultural evenings featuring music, dance, art, fashion

- a school newspaper with articles in all the school languages, including community languages

- internet clubs, where pupils can carry out research using online sources and work together on producing news bulletins, cultural reports, sports reports and so on

- a school radio broadcast, podcast or video

- planning, cooking and eating a French meal

- an outdoor French boules tournament for a year group

- a debating club

- a simulated Eurovision Song Contest – groups performing in as many languages as possible, with pupils as judges awarding points and announcing results in several languages

- a murder mystery evening, in the target language (TL)

- an Edward de Bono Six Thinking Hats® session, in a MFL. Edward de Bono has written a series of teacher resource books based on his ideas. Each 'thinking hat' is a device to represent a different mode of thinking. The language used can be relatively simple: it is the creativity of the thinking that is sophisticated. Ideas from the teacher's book could be adapted for use in languages other than English.

- a visit to an art gallery (or virtual, online art work), planned with the art department (plus pupils studying both art and a language) with pre-teaching of suitable language: the Musée d'Orsay website has a series '*L'enfant, image d'artistes et réalités sociales*' that would enhance learning for pupils doing History and Art, as well as French.

None of these activities needs to be carried on in isolation from the classroom – it is much better if they are not. The whole class could view an excerpt from a movie, which will be shown at the DVD club. This would serve as preparation as well as motivation. Pupils could follow up the viewing by writing a summary or a review in class. Alternatively, able pupils could choose a scene from a movie and give a presentation to their class based on it, particularly if they were also doing a media studies course.

The school newspaper could also be rooted in classroom activity, with pupils doing their planning and preparation there. They could use some of their class time to meet with other pupils in their year to check progress or to check each others' writing. See Appendix 4.10, Managing a group project: a pupil's sheet, to accompany some of the above activities.

Chapters 5 and 6 have other examples of after-school and out-of-school enrichment.

Differentiation – the concept

Differentiation is . . . recognizing [sic] individual differences and trying to find institutional strategies which take account of them. (. . .) It is not possible to differentiate for all children all the time – true differentiation is an aspiration – however, that does not negate the need to strive for improvement.

(Eyre 1997: 38–39)

As Eyre goes on to point out, not all differentiation happens as a result of planning, but because a teacher spots an opportunity. The teacher is the most expensive resource in the classroom – and the scarcest resource for an individual pupil. Often, more able pupils don't ask for help. Teachers assume able pupils can get on by themselves. But more able pupils are as entitled to as much teacher time as the less able. A brief word one-to-one can move a pupil forward – as the work of Vygotsky (see Chapter 3) showed:

> A judicious intervention of the teacher to urge pupils to a higher level of knowledge, skill, understanding and thinking was crucial.
>
> HMI Education Observed: The education of very able children
> in maintained schools (1992: viii)

Differentiation – the practice

Consider how to build in teacher time, using classroom layout and well-established routines to keep low-level demands on the teacher to a minimum, using in-class support and resources in general. A wall display – say in the form of a diagram or map, with 'have you checked/tried?' prompts – that pupils can consult to show steps to take when stuck would be an example. Teacher time with more able pupils can then be spent helping them to recognise their own and others' high level achievement and how to reuse their newly acquired expertise in a different situation. Teaching able pupils how to do paired evaluation, using pieces of work for sample evaluations, will help them become independent learners. In theory, at least, this will in turn free more teacher time. This model accords with the 'plan, do, review' model pupils will have used in design and technology. For able pupils especially, it is the planning and reviewing parts of the process that have the most potential for developing higher order thinking skills. These ideas are adapted from Eyre (1997: 55–56).

Here are some examples of how to use various differentiation strategies to challenge the more able cohort:

Task

An example from the 'in-depth listening' lesson plan (Appendix 4.6) is that pupils could try to memorise the first verse or the whole song. Other tasks, for example, activity 6 in the plan, require use of higher order thinking skills. Another challenging task would be to read one full-length book per term (or half-term or week!) in the TL.

Outcome

Pupils could be asked to produce a full page of writing, or more than one solution to a problem, or an extended talk.

Support

Pupils have to devise their own way of tackling a topic and preparing to present it to the class.

Time

Pupils who are learning their second (or third) MFL (for example, moving from French to Italian or Spanish) can be introduced to a range of verbs and tenses in a short time, because they will have already covered the complex concepts of verb formation and tense use in their first MFL. Advanced learners of Mandarin taking up Japanese (or vice versa) will already be able to read some of the characters those languages share.

Resource

Pupils can use A level texts, or websites, normally targeted at older students or adults.

Interest

Pupils can choose between a range of texts or recorded material according to their tastes; they can read about their hobby, but in the TL.

Learning style and differentiation

Learning style is also a tool for differentiation. It involves using different provision for individual needs. Representing the same body of information in a visual, audio-visual, kinaesthetic way would give certain pupils access to concepts they might otherwise miss. There is no implication here that teachers should be presenting a given topic in ways to fit a complete range of intelligences. Howard Gardner (1997) says, 'You can say that a child is a visual learner, but that's not a multiple intelligences way of talking about things. What I would say is, "Here is a child who very easily represents things spatially, and we can draw upon that strength if need be when we want to teach the child something new."' If the pupil seems to be struggling with a new concept, it may be helpful to say, 'What if we tried to put this in a (musical, theatrical, diagrammatic . . .) way?' Refer to Chapter 3 and multiple intelligences in the languages classroom for a variety of tasks on one topic intended to exploit pupils' individual strengths.

There are further lesson plans in the appendices which illustrate the above principles.

Lesson beginnings and endings

Having spent some time looking at the main content of a lesson, we move on to looking at its bookends. In its message to do with pedagogical skills, the QCA has focused attention on 'starters' and 'plenaries' as separate entities worth examining in their own right.

Starters

One crucial factor in designing quick-start activities for a MFL lesson is that it should be obvious what the pupil is being asked to do.

For two examples in context, see Appendix 4.2 Starter activity for lesson within Year 8 Unit 11 topic *A la mode* and Appendix 4.4 Lesson to revise past tense formation: starter exercise.

Here are a few others, which can be made more demanding for more able pupils, or which could contain mini-extensions:

- Generating a list or a mind map

- Finding the French/Spanish/Japanese for . . . (based on a reading passage)

- Putting a set of phrases/words into an order that makes sense

- A list of phrases/sentences – which is correct, which is not?

- Matching questions and answers

- Breaking up a 'wordworm' – a long sentence that has not been separated into words – and making one up for a partner to decode

- Finding the odd one out (e.g. odd sound out: *bonjour*, **chanson**, *jamais*, *magique*, *mangeons*) – including familiar and unfamiliar words

- Finding the opposite: *un grand château confortable mais froid; une réponse compliquée mais incorrecte; un vieil homme sincère mais un peu intolérant; un petit pays pauvre mais magnifique – ajoutez deux autres exemples si vous avez le temps*

- Playing noughts and crosses: each square contains a phrase (noun + adjective; noun + verb; mini-sentence) – pairs of pupils could compete to see who gets a line first.

Plenaries

For more able pupils, these should focus on thinking about key points or key words, summarising the lesson, re-stating the purpose of the lesson, recalling stages, thinking up questions for others (to test whether the learning objectives have been met), thinking about how they have learned, or how the lesson links to their previous or future learning.

- more able pupils (pairs, or singly) could take the 'hot seat' to answer questions about the lesson – or make up questions to ask someone else

- pupils could give examples to show what they have learned – or share these with their partner

- pupils could write/compose a two-point summary of the lesson

- pupils could rate themselves on their comprehension of the main points of the lesson and give feedback.

Skills needed by the most able and ways of developing them

Just looking at the skills that feature in the highest National Curriculum level descriptions and how to nurture them from Year 7 (or the moment a pupil first encounters a MFL) is a good way of approaching planning, although it is daunting. Bear in mind that these descriptions could also be applied to final-year university students or an expert linguist. Many native speakers would not meet these targets! A sense of proportion is required: we are talking about what could be achieved by an exceptional 14–16 year old. It is helpful to begin by considering the two skills that emphasise comprehension. Pupils need to be able to decode and analyse material if they are to model their own language on it.

Attainment target 1: Listening and responding

Level 8 – Pupils show that they understand different types of spoken material from a range of sources (for example, news items, interviews, documentaries, films and plays). When listening to familiar and less familiar material they draw inferences, recognise attitudes and emotions, and need little repetition.

Exceptional performance – Pupils show that they understand a wide range of factual and imaginative speech, some of which expresses different points of view, issues and concerns. They summarise in detail, report, and explain extracts, orally and in writing. They develop their independent listening by selecting from and responding to recorded sources according to their interests.

Planning for development of excellent listening skills

If we take the key ideas from these descriptions, we can check that suitable experiences and a 'wide range' are presented over a period of time of, say, one year. The planning grid below is a suggested way forward.

This grid, without the final column, could even be issued to exceptionally able and/or well-motivated pupils, or bilingual pupils, as a checklist for their own use. The checklist could also be used to inform a mentor. Feedback from the pupil could add to and improve the list of resources – for the benefit of others.

Fewer activities that are well exploited and leave pupils feeling more confident and competent are better than a large number that serve only to make the listener feel inadequate.

Preparation for in-depth listening

- Choose something pupils will want to listen to – if it is funny or there is a mystery to it, or music with it, it will be more enjoyable and memorable. A high-flying (Physics) graduate of the prestigious École Polytechnique now speaks fluent, idiomatic English – he claims he learned it all from having spent hours as a teenager listening to English pop songs.

- Give some clues to what the extract is about, then elicit what vocabulary pupils already know and what they know of the issues/topic under discussion.

What pupils need to do	Keywords	Typical practice material	Resources	Place in s.o.w.	Example	Help
show understanding, explain	a range of sources: factual	news	Internet BBCi radio TV Authentik		*Education Guardian* language resources	consortium
infer		interviews	radio, TV		musicians in *Buena Vista Social Club*	
summarise		documentaries			extract from documentary on over-fishing	local university
recognise attitudes and emotions	imaginative	films plays poetry, song	DVDs A level text book		scene from *Les 400 Coups* poem: '*Le Déserteur*'	
develop independent listening		what they are interested in	any recorded sources		bbc.co.uk/languages has audio with transcripts; songs & exercises	FLA recommendations, penfriend, website

Planning grid: developing excellent listening skills

- Pre-teach some key vocabulary. This can make a big difference to the quality of listening or listening and watching – for example, before viewing a film extract.

Other points worth considering

- Some transferable higher level skills are used in listening: the pupil will be practising the skills of inferring, summarising, reporting and explaining, for example, in other subjects and contexts. However, they will still need practice in the TL.

- To be able to 'recognise attitudes and emotions', the linguistic knowledge required is the set of exclamations and patterns of intonation that would accompany humour, happiness/sadness, pleasure/anger, irony, sarcasm, surprise, boredom, indifference, fear and defiance. A good question would be: 'How does this person feel and how do you know?'

- Some useful language will also arise (for example, to do with expressing emotion) in work on the skills of writing and speaking, thus reinforcing what is required for listening.

- Listening to a barrage of spoken foreign language can make huge demands on short-term memory, thus arousing anxiety, feelings of inadequacy and causing stress. This is not motivating at all. So, do allow pupils to work collaboratively on decoding the language and answering the questions. This will help them share the 'processing load' and feel less stressed, as well as getting all the other benefits associated with collaborative learning (see Vygotsky, Chapter 3).

- One of the lesson plans in the appendices (see 4.5 – notes – and 4.6 – plan) centres on developing high level listening skills in French. The plan could serve as a model for exploiting similar recorded material in another language.

Attainment target 3: Reading and responding

Level 8 – Pupils show that they understand a wide variety of types of written material. When reading for personal interest and for information, they consult a range of reference sources where appropriate. They cope readily with unfamiliar topics involving more complex language, and recognise attitudes and emotions.

Exceptional performance – Pupils show that they understand a wide range of factual and imaginative texts, some of which express different points of view, issues and concerns, and which include official and formal material. They summarise in detail, report, and explain extracts, orally and in writing. They develop their independent reading by choosing stories, articles, books and plays according to their interests, and responding to them.

Again, a planning grid can help – and can be shared with pupils where appropriate. See Appendix 4.8 for Planning grid: developing excellent reading skills.

The other two attainment targets focus on production of language and therefore require similar skills. The development of excellent 'productive skills' of writing and speaking can grow out of well-selected reading and listening models, as well as the examples provided 'live' by the teacher and FLA. It may be simpler to extend the listening and reading grids to include linked speaking/writing work that covers:

- 'a wide range of factual and imaginative topics'

- 'formal/informal situations'

- how to 'develop content'

- how to 'justify ideas'

- 'unpredictable elements in conversations'

- what constitutes 'coherence'.

Different terminology from the above, as teachers know, will be used for a high level performance in languages such as Russian, Japanese and Mandarin.

Higher order skills

Bloom's taxonomy

This often-cited system is particularly worth bearing in mind when considering challenge for more able pupils. Bloom (1956) identified six levels of thinking, given here in hierarchical order, beginning with the simplest. Since teachers need to use certain types of questions in order to prompt thinking at higher levels, there are examples of matching questions in a MFL:

- knowledge (recalling information): '*qu'est-ce que c'est?*' + flashcard; numbers, days of week

- comprehension (giving meaning to information): '*c'est dans le présent ou dans le passé?*'

- application (using knowledge, for example, to solve problems): '*mettez ces événements dans le bon ordre*'

- analysis (to take complex knowledge apart in order to understand it better): '*comparez ces deux personnages*'

- synthesis (putting together, to create something new): '*prenez le point de vue d'un des personnages de cette histoire et racontez ce qui s'est passé et pourquoi*'

- evaluation (assessing, judging): '*comparez deux films: lequel serait meilleur pour regarder en classe et pourquoi?*'

Within these levels, it is also possible to provide further differentiation by 'requiring from some children more knowledge, more specialised knowledge, deeper understanding, more examples ... more detailed analysis' or by allocating certain tasks to particular pupils while they are working with their peers on a group-work activity (Leyden 1998: 59–60).

Asking questions

Recently the late E. C. Wragg, D. Brown and their team carried out some valuable research, analysis and writing about the key professional skill of asking questions. How do their findings relate to the more able and to MFL? Firstly, the subject is complicated in MFL because questions can be asked in English or in the target language. Clearly, asking a high level question in the TL will not serve any purpose unless the pupil's competence is quite high. While it is highly desirable to practise the TL as much as possible in a lesson, the 2000 version of the MFL programme of study requires that teachers and pupils deal with grammar points explicitly. They will have to discuss them in English at times, but this discussion will give the MFL teacher a good opportunity not only to ask questions that require pupils to analyse, synthesise and evaluate, but also to use technical terms.

Regardless of what language is being used for questioning, it is certainly worth looking at what Wragg and Brown call 'tactics'. MFL teachers who have put together an effective set of questions to ask in an oral examination will already be proficient in most of these tactics, so we will start with those. In order to elicit the pupil's best performance in an examination, the teacher/examiner has to take great care to:

- set the context (verbally) for a sequence of questions, or signal a change of subject

- ask open rather than closed (yes/no) questions

- judge whether to put the next question or to allow the pupil to elaborate (i.e. use pauses effectively)

- keep the pace comfortable but not too comfortable

- gauge the 'register', so that the pupil does not misunderstand

- prompt without supplying the answer or undermining the pupil's confidence and flow

- ask for examples, opinions, clarification, reasons

- listen carefully (thinking about what to ask next), supportively and encouragingly

- plan a logical sequence of questions

- enable pupils to feel comfortable about putting their own questions (for clarification, say)

- resist the urge to ask too many questions, but keep the balance of the exchanges so that the pupil does most of the speaking.

The principles in the classroom are the same, except that the questions will be spread over a set of pupils. A 'no hands' classroom convention allows the teacher to direct the questions so as to involve the whole class and to choose who receives which question (higher level questions for more able pupils). Another technique is to pause for a short 'pair and share' session: pairs of pupils discuss how they would answer and can then give a more polished, confident answer.

Quick questions

In a class situation, questions are the quickest way of assessing what stage the pupils have reached in their thinking. At the beginning of a lesson, the teacher can use them to recap points covered previously or take homework feedback. After quick-fire practice in the TL to recall material from the previous lesson, the teacher can judge whether to direct a particular group of pupils to move on to the next (differentiated) task while others have further practice. A vague or evasive answer, however, needs to be followed up: Has the pupil not understood? Does s/he need help expressing the concept? Does s/he need to be challenged to look more deeply at the problem?

If the class is practising the MFL orally, the teacher may work quickly to 'prime the pump' of language flow, creating a feeling of enjoyment and competence, then gradually narrow the focus, slow the pace, pose a more demanding question and then pause to give pupils more time, saying: 'You've got a minute to think about this before I'll start taking answers.' This pause allows pupils to reflect so as to produce answers of better quality and/or length.

Building on pupils' answers

If pupil A's answer is not quite right, the teacher can choose not to correct it, but to ask pupil B, and even C, before returning to pupil A, who will often have been able to self-correct, from having listened attentively to B and C. The teacher could alternatively ask the class their opinion on the best answer.

At the end of the lesson, the teacher can come back to particular answers and show how they contributed to the learning that took place. Sometimes a wrong answer is the best thing to learn from – a point worth making!

Finally, and most importantly, if 'key' questions are identified as an integral part of the lesson plan, there is a better chance that the lesson will have focus. To identify these key questions, Wragg and Brown recommend using a mind map (there is an example in Chapter 4) and conclude with some practical and encouraging advice:

it is worth pointing out that most teachers find preparing topics or themes easier than preparing specific lessons, for a topic or theme is a meaningful chunk in one's own head, but the individual lessons may not be so clear. Hence, there is much to be said in favour of preparing sets of lessons on a topic using mind maps, GAITO (Goals, Activities, Input, Timing, Order) and key questions.

(Wragg and Brown 2001: 67)

A training module on the subtle art of questioning, Module 4 of Training materials for the Foundation Subjects (DfES 0350/2002, found on the Standards website www.standards.dfes.gov.uk) could be used within the department as INSET.

Homework

This is one of the best means of individualising the curriculum, especially for the more able. As with all pupils, doing homework should be a way of reinforcing what has been done in the classroom and doing private practice on skills such as speaking and reading aloud. It should as far as possible involve doing things that pupils will want to do. If it involves rote learning of vocabulary or verb forms, pupils should not only know how to ensure that the information goes into their long-term memory, but how to memorise efficiently – maybe they can think of a game or strategy that will help other pupils too.

Model a homework task such as private listening to create good habits for lifelong language learning. Pupils need to know that building a repertoire of language that will move them to another level of competence requires effort. It is very similar to learning to play a musical instrument or to snowboard well. Unless pupils are actively engaged in some way while they are doing homework tasks, the time they spend will not have any long-term benefits.

Model private reading in a similar way. A high-flying linguist may enjoy reading a full-length book, say, over a month or a half term. S/he can keep a diary or reading log to record reading sessions, measure progress and keep track of queries to discuss with the teacher, FLA or mentor. One gifted linguist, at age 15, found the *Petit Nicolas* series, with its lively illustrations by Sempé, appealed perfectly to her sense of humour.

Depending on the age and level of the pupils, the department can gradually allow them more choice over the way they present homework. Pupils could:

- produce a Venn diagram or mind map (of a concept or list of expressions/vocabulary)
- create a storyboard
- write an essay
- write/devise a role-play
- create a tape/video recording

- create a PowerPoint presentation

- create a diagram

- create a flow chart

- write a song, a poem, a rap

- do a cartoon strip

- make a poster.

For the able all-rounder, it is worth trying to think of ways of overlapping subjects and skills, since these pupils are likely to be the most time-poor. There is a case study of such a pupil (Chloe) in Chapter 5. Encourage pupils to think creatively about cross-curricular links and come up with suggestions. One of the exciting moments for a MFL teacher happens when pupils recycle their research work in a subject they are passionate about: they write and speak about it in one – or two or three – other languages. One able pupil took what he learned in an art course about the development of perspective in Italian painting as a topic for his Italian speaking test.

Recording and assessment for multiple intelligences

Just as schools are finding imaginative tasks for homework, so they are developing a range of ways of tracking pupils' progress and involving pupils in tracking themselves. Where pupils have difficulty producing written work, they may be able to use voice recognition software or 'talk' the task while someone else records in writing.

A quote from Howard Gardner (1997) makes a good guiding principle: 'let's always allow students to show their understanding in a variety of ways.' Different tasks, such as those suggested in Chapter 3 for using multiple intelligences in the languages classroom, could be used as a basis for assessment, whether written or not. It is useful to get together with a colleague from another department to devise criteria that fit. For example, since much MFL pupils' work in the early stages leads to the production of art work, one MFL teacher consulted the art department and set up suitable criteria to distinguish between some wonderful pieces of work entered for a MFL competition. The art teacher was one of the judges. This was seen to be fair by pupils and made MFL staff more confident about their skills when judging visual presentations.

A similar collaboration has taken place between a drama and MFL department at Islington Green School, using assessment for learning with extended role-plays.

Where pupils are using non-linguistic skills to enhance MFL projects, then, it makes sense to use non-linguistic criteria as part of the assessment. It is important to share (or devise) the criteria with pupils as tasks are being set, so that they are clear in advance that – even if non-linguistic skills are being given credit – more weight will be given to linguistic ones.

Portfolios

Portfolios, mentioned in Chapter 2, are ways of helping pupils keep a record of their languages achievements and are gaining credence as reliable assessment tools. The European Language Portfolio, launched in 2001, is a personal languages portfolio that records pupils' language learning and cultural experiences. Its three parts are: the Passport (an overview of proficiency and record of assessment), a Language Biography and a Dossier or collection of materials and achievements. CILT has information on this project: www.cilt.org.uk.

Records of achievement

These are well established in most schools. Some schools now have intranets set up so that such records are becoming easier to compose and update.

Other vehicles for assessment

User-friendly technology is now making it possible to use new media such as video to record individual performances and presentations for assessment. For many pupils, there is something intrinsically motivating about performing in front of a camera. Video playbacks – as a means of analysing and improving performance – are becoming more common. Therefore it makes sense (and will make sense to pupils) to use them in the languages domain. Our pupils are growing up in a visual culture; they are comfortable with new technology and able to discriminate between those who present well and less well on the screen. It is not a big step for them to take to become perceptive judges of languages skills (along with certain other skills – they can help to decide which). This is a good opportunity to practise assessment for learning, for teacher and pupil.

Teachers should also work towards empowering pupils to carry out self-evaluations and setting their own targets. The most effective evaluation and target-setting is short-term. Self-evaluation can be used at a group level, such as when a group is carrying out a project. Most of the enrichment activities listed in this chapter could have an evaluation aspect built in, to provide feedback to pupils as well as staff.

Endnote

To return to Leyden's words at the beginning of the chapter, 'teaching is a highly skilled and demanding activity' and it sometimes seems to classroom teachers that they are expected to cure all the ills of society as well as teach. It is understandable that teachers should develop 'initiative fatigue'. So it is not easy to write about the fascinating and powerful research (by others) that underpins the ideas in this chapter, without thinking that all this production of ideas does not necessarily make classroom life easier for the MFL teacher. Some initiatives have: the Literacy Strategy and the closer attention being paid to language structure in the primary school relieve the MFL department from its previous role of being the only department to have to teach concepts such as 'the adverb' to pupils. The work of the MFL department ought now, therefore, to have more in common with – and receive reinforcement from – work going on in other subject areas. However, what goes on in the classroom is still amazingly complex. This chapter cannot simplify such a complex process, but it should have helped to give your department some ideas that they 'with care and imagination' can use to benefit their able pupils.

Summary

- The department should work towards using a planning model which best meets the needs of all its pupils but explicitly includes the most able cohort.

- Enrichment is the principal means of providing for the needs of the more able.

- Enrichment opportunities are many and varied.

- Good differentiation (catering for individual differences) can be planned but is often the result of close observation (assessment) by the teacher.

- Look ahead to what constitutes an excellent performance in languages and begin early to build the necessary skills.

- Think about questions that challenge able pupils to use higher order skills.

- Plan a few key questions that will give direction to a lesson.

- Plan to set interesting homework and teach able pupils how to use homework time well.

- Building a departmental bank of ideas for good starters and plenaries is a worthwhile ongoing project.

- New technology and ideas offer a range of ways of tracking pupils' learning.

CHAPTER 5

Supporting the learning of more able pupils

- Support for more able pupils with learning difficulties
- Working with the SENCO
- Case study: an able linguist with visual impairment
- Case study: an able linguist with cerebral palsy (CP)
- Case studies: able linguists with special educational needs
- Case study: an able pupil with ADHD
- Case study: an able pupil with Asperger syndrome
- Providing support in school: teaching assistants
- Liaising with the pastoral team
- Study support outside school hours
- Mentors – who are they and what is their role?
- Case study: an exceptionally gifted and talented pupil
- The school library/resource and learning centre
- Links with parents/carers
- Liaising with external agencies

This chapter looks at learning support: those resources centred on the school which can provide practical and emotional support for the special needs of the more able MFL learner. Some children will need specialist support throughout their school careers; others will need intervention at certain times.

Support for more able pupils with learning difficulties

We look first at definitions of special educational needs. An able linguist could also have the following special needs:

- cognition and learning needs:
  - pupils with specific learning difficulties (SpLD) – for example, dyslexia
- behavioural, emotional and social development needs (BESD):
  - pupils with emotional and behavioural difficulties, for example, those individuals who are withdrawn or isolated or disruptive
  - pupils with attention deficit disorder (ADD)
  - pupils with attention deficit hyperactivity disorder (ADHD)
- communication and interaction needs:
  - pupils with autistic spectrum disorder (ASD) or Asperger syndrome
  - pupils with hearing (HI), visual (VI) and/or physical (PD) impairment.

Working with the SENCO

With these pupils, it will be important to liaise with the special educational needs coordinator (SENCO) for particular strategies that have been effective and to formulate ways of working with support staff. If the department has nominated a member of staff to have special responsibility for SEN, that person should maintain regular contact (meetings, memos or a combination of both) with the SENCO.

It is very important to remember that every person with special needs is different and to work with their strengths. Labels or diagnostic criteria are guidelines only. If they are taken too literally, they can limit a person's potential.

Pupils with HI, VI and PD will vary enormously in what support they need. With a visually impaired pupil, for example, strategies will depend on how the pupil sees. Some pupils can read in extreme close-up, while others will use enlarged print or a CCTV. In the classroom, seating position is very important. Issues such as lighting and glare need to be considered. Forward planning is also essential, so that the pupil always has the necessary materials. Flashcards can still be used for certain partially-sighted pupils, provided they are held close enough. Dictionary use is problematic, as the required scanning and skimming can be physically wearing for some pupils. Consider using a CD dictionary, and 'talking text' or a laptop with a bilingual talking dictionary installed. Continual technological development ought to enhance the language-learning opportunities for these pupils in the long term.

Case study: an able linguist with visual impairment

Jody (Year 10)

Jody is an academically able all-rounder who is particularly keen on French. She attended a primary school which had a unit with expertise in enabling children with visual impairments to work in ordinary classrooms, and from there moved to a similarly equipped secondary school. She can read close up but only by holding a page up to her eye. Print on dark or coloured background is even more difficult for her; on a computer screen she prefers white on a black background. She can see at a distance by using a small telescope to reduce a panorama to a manageable size. Possibly because of the limitations in her vision, she has developed a formidable memory and has excellent listening skills. Her parents are keen for her to take as full a part in school activities, including sports, as possible. She is therefore impressively confident, has good social skills and is well-liked by her peers. Furthermore, she is often able to help staff find ways round her limitations. She has a laptop computer and has developed good keyboard skills. Jody has been on a school trip to Paris. So that she could look at a painted ceiling, a member of staff helped her to point her telescope in the right direction. She was able to 'see' the sights by capturing views using a small digital camera.

Strategies

- Make sure that colleagues are aware of the nature of her visual impairment because this will influence the choice of support strategies.

- Give careful thought to where she should sit in the classroom.

- Liaise with the SEN team over reading materials. Use of either a CCTV or enlarged print will have to be set up in advance. Some text may be more accessible if it is scanned and then enlarged, to be displayed on a screen or on white paper. To decrease the physical demands on Jody, select higher level text and give her in-depth work on a smaller amount of material.

- Flashcard images can be transferred to her laptop. Jody's learning buddy or the support teacher can help navigate through the set that is being displayed to the rest of the class. Use white on black wherever possible.

- Get the FLA to record the reading passages on Jody's digital voice recorder (this may actually be one of the functions built into her mobile phone). When she needs to refer to it to model her writing, a recorded version may be physically easier for her to work with.

- A CD version of a dictionary should be made available to Jody for use both in and out of lessons.

Case study: an able linguist with cerebral palsy (CP)

Selina (Year 7)

Selina is an academically able all-rounder who is particularly keen on Spanish. In her primary school, a support unit facilitated the integration of children with physical disabilities into mainstream education. She was identified as having high ability, although her speech was rather slow. She moves around the school with some difficulty and cannot, for example, carry her books to lessons. She can write accurately and imaginatively in English and has taken to Spanish with enthusiasm. Her speech can be unclear, for example, towards the end of a long sentence. However, her close friends understand her easily. Selina has a good sense of humour and an excellent memory.

Strategies

- Make sure that colleagues are aware of the implications of her disability because this will influence the choice of support strategies.

- Keep lines of communication open so that Selina and her family feel free to contribute any useful information.

- Provide helpful seating arrangements, so that it is physically easy to access the necessary materials.

- If it is necessary to decrease physical demands on Selina, cut down on the amount she is expected to produce, or look for creative ways of maximising her learning opportunities.

- Consult the SEN coordinator for specialist equipment, physical needs, and make sure the MFL department has access to what is needed for every lesson, including a word processing package with accents and possibly an electronic dictionary. A laptop and an interactive CD would also be helpful for home use.

- Model appropriate communication strategies for other pupils to adopt: allow extra time for listening to Selina, so as not to devalue her contribution.

- As Selina's fellow pupils learn how to counteract prejudice and discrimination, allow them to assume the role of facilitator, while monitoring their behaviour.

- Be on the lookout for a learning buddy in Spanish, but switch partners for certain activities, to allow others to interact with Selina.

- Chorus work and repetition will give opportunities for practising speaking in a less stressful way. As with Jody (above), consider using a digital voice recorder to support home practice in listening, speaking and writing.

- Refer to Scope (www.scope.org.uk) for specialist information if necessary.

Case studies: able linguists with special educational needs

Michael – Dyslexic (Year 9)

Michael obtained a place at a boys' grammar school but has struggled ever since. He has an extensive vocabulary and always volunteers for drama productions and reporting back when working in a group. He enjoys music, art and D&T, and brings a keen imagination and wit to all these subjects. Michael prefers the company of teachers and older pupils with whom he likes to debate topical issues. His peers, on the other hand, regard him as a 'bit of a wimp' as he does not enjoy sport and frequently corrects their behaviour.

After a very slow start in early childhood, Michael can now read fluently but his other problems associated with dyslexia remain. His spelling and handwriting are very poor. He finds it almost impossible to obtain information from large swathes of text. Even when the main ideas are summarised for him in bullet points, he still has difficulty revising for examinations or tests or picking out and organising the main points for an essay. In maths, he is criticised for the chaotic layout of his work but he finds it difficult to organise things in a way that is logical to other people. His family is very supportive and gives him a lot of help with homework, so much so that teachers are sometimes misled into believing that he is coping well, until his difficulties are highlighted by his very poor performance in written exams.

Because he is so articulate, Michael is able to explain his frustrations to his teachers who are, on the whole, sympathetic. However, they are not very helpful in providing him with useful strategies.

Strategies

- Liaise with the SEN team so that your approach with Michael fits in with their overall support programme for him: for example, providing uncluttered reading materials; teaching him to apply the skimming and scanning skills he has learned in English.

- Teach Michael to mind map so that he can use this skill to record information and revise if he finds this helpful. Adding colour and pictures may also work.

- Spell out links between sound and the written form in the target language, even using English sounds where this is helpful: *qu'est-ce que c'est* = keskesay.

- Encourage Michael to remember vocabulary/sentences by making audio recordings or setting them to music. Copying from the board is time-consuming and difficult for him – it will be better to give him a printed list of vocabulary (which could be in the form of a table with certain items missing, say, for him to complete – or a mind map of the topic).

- For learning vocabulary and verb forms he could also use verb game cards, highlighters, Post-its.

- Make sure that homework tasks are suitable for his level of ability but are modified to allow him to succeed (by asking him to tape his answers, rather than write them, for example). For grammar topics, always give examples with every 'rule'.

- Make use of his willingness to act as a reporter to build up his speaking skills in the TL.

- Encourage him to word process some homework; help him find a word processing package that copes with accents: http://french.typeit.org/, http://german.typeit.org/, http://spanish.typeit.org/ and http://italian.typeit.org/ will help if he is emailing or able to work online.

- Suggest he uses a spreadsheet package for his writing as a way of organising his ideas in written form: grouping arguments on a topic in 3 columns (for/against/neutral); taking items (vocabulary/expressions) in a reading passage, pasting them into 3 columns, known/guessable/not known.

- Give him a key, wherever possible, so that he can correct his own work.

- Encourage him to work with a 'study buddy.'

- Provide scripts to go with listening materials (preferably CDs, which are easier to navigate than tapes).

- Encourage him to read about successful linguists with dyslexia on www.hull.ac.uk/languages/about_us/support/dyslexia/guidline_dyslexia/case_study/index.html.

Example project

Get Michael to act as the director of a series of role-plays about the local area/environment, with various characters giving opposite opinions on its good and bad points and ways of improving it. Video it. Michael and his group could put together a whiteboard presentation with photos and commentary, showing good and bad points about the area.

Case study: an able pupil with ADHD

Trevor (Year 8)

Trevor had the highest aggregated CATs score when he entered his comprehensive school but was described by his primary teachers as having a 'self-destruct button'. He is a bundle of contradictions. On good days he is capable of being charming and polite. Sometimes he becomes so engrossed in an activity that it is hard to draw him away from it. He loves books, especially those with detailed maps and diagrams, and likes to share what he has found out with teachers and other adults. He is a natural actor and sings and looks like an angel.

Yet Trevor is equally capable of destroying a lesson with his extremely disruptive and increasingly dangerous behaviour. He will erupt from his chair and turn on a machine just as someone puts their hands near it. His science teachers have had to give up all practical lessons and lock the preparation room when he is around because he uses his intelligence and wide reading to destructive effect. He has an intense dislike of writing and rarely does class work or submits homework. In mental arithmetic he excels although he is reluctant to allow classmates many opportunities to show what they know.

For a small band of troublesome peers, he is a hero. Most other pupils laugh at his antics but find him very disturbing. They are rarely brave enough to offer criticism.

His mother will not acknowledge that there is a problem and refuses to consider medication or psychiatric help.

Strategies

- Investigate the possibility that he is also dyslexic if this has not already been done. Also, his cognitive style may be 'wholist' (see Chapter 3): he will therefore need a clear structure for his behaviour. Similarly, when learning, he will need help with breaking a situation down into its parts although he will easily see the big picture. Riding (2002: 63) points out that 'investigations of pupils referred to special schools (EBD) show that male wholists and verbalisers are in the majority'.

- Agree on a school wide policy of support, and even containment. In the classroom, practise clear routines, address Trevor by name, insist on eye contact, choose seating carefully.

- Prioritise what behaviour or work is to be achieved and put in place a reward system. It might be best to make no demands as far as written work is concerned until the behaviour has been dealt with.

- Consider a 'learning buddy'; if using group work, choose a subgroup where Trevor can take a leading role and where someone else is the scribe.

- Try to capitalise on his acting ability by praising his ability to mimic and use him as a model for pronunciation – get him to demonstrate.

- Get him – and all the class – to be 'time-aware', by giving instructions 'start now'; 'in 2 minutes we will be . . .' (in the target language) and check that these signals have been understood.

- Invite his mother to sit in on some lessons where the problems are most severe and keep trying to work with her.

Example project – give him a choice:

- Finding a good reading book in French and explaining why he likes it.

- On a website (see resources section), finding a traditional song in French that tells a story, suitable for the class to sing. Teaching his group the words – taping it, playing it to the class, and leading his group in teaching it to the rest of the class. Get help from the music teacher, ICT teacher, Learning Support where/if necessary.

- Reading part of Harry Potter in French. Practising reading it until it sounds really good (practising with the FLA, if possible); recording it. Putting together a PowerPoint show with illustrations and the recorded reading, so that other pupils can understand.

- Trevor could research ADHD/ADD on the ADDNET UK website – perhaps – when he's more mature.

Case study: an able pupil with Asperger syndrome

Malcolm (Year 7)

In spite of careful liaison between the primary school and the head of Year 7, teachers were still taken by surprise when they met Malcolm. They had not appreciated that he would have to be taught many things that other children pick up by observation. For instance, he did not understand about queuing for his lunch and simply crawled between everyone's legs to get to the food.

His speech is robotic and it can be disconcerting when he does not give the expected answer. He does not understand tact and might say, 'That dress is old' without appreciating that this could give offence. Sometimes he becomes obsessed by a door or window and wants it opened to a particular angle. This same obsession is apparent in his written work where he can become anxious if teachers try to persuade him to set it out in a different way.

He is a very able mathematician and should reach university level in three or four years. However, he cannot cope with group work or group investigations and will become quite agitated if put into such a situation. Malcolm is also an outstanding chess player and was representing the school within a few weeks of arriving. In all other academic subjects he copes quite well in the top set although his very literal understanding of some concepts can create problems, particularly in English.

Sport is a mystery to him. He does not understand the rules and is, in any case, lumbering and ungainly. It is during these lessons that his peers are most likely to be unkind, although, on the whole, they are quite protective towards him.

Strategies

- Use the whole-school support system. There should be coordinated support for Malcolm across the school. One person should be responsible for monitoring him on a regular basis.

- Bear in mind that Asperger syndrome is a developmental disorder which implies that skills are learned at a slower rate, but that they can be learned.

- Teach any social skills he lacks in a very simple and direct way, for example, 'When someone says "How are you?" you say, "Fine, thank you".' Teach the same basic skills when practising in the target language. Elicit features of non-verbal communication from other pupils. Get other pupils to practise with Malcolm, for example, standing at an appropriate distance, looking the person in the eye while speaking to them.

- When the class is working in groups, Malcolm could try working as part of a pair, where he has a specific task to accomplish that does not demand long periods of interaction. Encourage his partner and him to find a device they can use to determine whose turn it is to talk and whose it is to listen. Don't expect him to join in language games unless he has had time to understand the rules (preferably written down) – maybe he could be the time keeper, for example (using target language).

- Find a suitable place where he can get a break from sensory overload from time to time (and suitable activities to do on his own). If there is a quiet corner in the IT room, he could play chess online for a time. One school gave a child with Asperger syndrome a role as a helper in the library so that she had a quiet place to be during break.

- Make classroom routines explicit and say why. Flag up any changes ahead of time: 'next lesson we will be . . .' and ask Malcolm to repeat what he has understood to check the message got through. If there is a teaching assistant in the class, they can do this checking.

- Consider some one-to-one help such as a mentor – a TL-speaking university student who also has an interest in chess, for example.

- Encourage other pupils to be proud of his achievements for the school when he plays in the chess team. Try to set up e-mail with other chess players; encourage him to read about chess on websites in the target language and to write about his games in the TL.

- If Malcolm is to go on a school trip abroad, get his parents' input about his routines and triggers – for example, avoiding certain colours. He will need someone there who can troubleshoot (his parents may have to accompany him).

- Give him the chance to do things for himself and make his own choices: for example, let him adjust the window himself and say: 'Do you want to do it?' (in the TL).

Example project

Malcolm can research the lives of some famous mathematicians and/or physicists and present their stories in French – either in writing, if he prefers, or in oral form. Set up a short session for him with the foreign language assistant, to practise intonation and get him to record himself at home and bring the recording in for the FLA to listen to.

If the group is doing a project such as putting together a newspaper, he could act as editor and correct others' work.

Providing support in school: teaching assistants

There are various names for the support staff who are employed to help pupils with special needs or for general classroom support. Some of the ways a teaching assistant (TA) can be used in the MFL classroom, with more able pupils, are:

- working with pupils with special needs or a group that includes an SEN pupil. It is important that the pupil with SEN is not over-dependent on a TA and that a TA is able to help other pupils

- preparing materials and ensuring that any support technology (recorder, viewer, laptop) is in place

- keeping records, helping/observing the pupil reach individual education plan (IEP) targets

- monitoring small-group work.

A TA attached to a year group can gain in-depth knowledge of particular pupils and can provide encouragement, troubleshoot, find ways of keeping them engaged.

The more the work of the support teacher is integrated into the work of the teacher or department, the better. Departments who have developed effective ways of managing TAs usually get a better share of these resources. In the best case scenario, the teacher or head of department have some regular joint planning time and are able to discuss each other's expectations and review their work.

A department may also use foreign language assistants (FLAs) for classroom support or for after-school activities. The usual way of locating a FLA is through the British Council. Unfortunately, many schools cannot afford a FLA on their own and are obliged to share one with a neighbouring school. Since it is hard to find a mutually satisfactory schedule, it may be better for schools that are close to a university to advertise there for suitable candidates. European university students who are studying for degrees in Britain are a good resource. Advantages of this system for the school are not only financial:

- the FLAs are employed by the hour

- the school sets its own rate of pay

- if FLAs are absent they are not paid

but also practical and educational:

- attendance is generally good: there is always a replacement available from a waiting list in case of unforeseen problems

- they will often make up time missed for an unavoidable absence

- students are not usually required to leave in the middle of term in order to take exams abroad

- timetables can be much more flexible, allowing for more pupils to work with FLAs, even when all GCSE classes are timetabled together

- they can be selected after they have been observed working with pupils in the classroom (as part of the interview process)

- FLAs often discover unexpected talents and a strong commitment to teaching

- FLAs are lively, energetic, fun, happy to have work and involvement in the community; they gain insights about their host culture that they will not otherwise have had

- a contact person at the university may be able to help with communication, recruitment and occasionally screening

- the flexibility of the scheme seems eminently suitable for providing for the needs of more able pupils.

A job description for a foreign language assistant is included as Appendix 5.1.

Through the Comenius project, a school can also host a visitor from abroad who contributes across the curriculum. Although the school can only host someone who speaks a language the school does not offer – in fact, priority is given to languages that are rarely taught in the UK – the MFL department can still benefit. In one case, a Greek assistant helped with a lunchtime languages club and also provided support and ideas in cookery lessons. See the British Council website www.britishcouncil.org for further information.

Liaising with the pastoral team

Form tutors and heads of year or other pastoral teachers are often able to spot problems, as they may be the first to receive messages from parents or carers, or realise that individual pupils are having problems over several subject areas. Some year tutors monitor additional workload stress where pupils are involved in special programmes. In schools where form tutors 'follow' their forms through to Year 11, they have the benefit of knowing the pupil over a few years and are therefore in a privileged position to pick up changes, suggest opportunities and so on. Form tutors can help, for example, by providing emotional support, showing they value an able pupil's achievement, or detecting problems such as isolation or bullying. They may also be able to propose ways of developing skills outside the usual curriculum areas. For example, they could suggest leadership roles for more able pupils, including pupils with behavioural difficulties: a more able pupil can give support to a less able pupil; a pupil with behavioural problems can supervise a younger pupil, say, in a chess club.

For pastoral–departmental communication to work, an easy-to-use system is a must. It could take the form of an update each term organised by the school coordinator. It could also happen that an informal 'word' – between the form tutor and MFL teacher – is enough to draw attention to a need or to provide a worthwhile idea.

Study support outside school hours

Study support (also known as 'out-of-school-hours learning' (OSHL)) is beginning to be more formalised and recognised – and resourced by the Government. A commonly used definition appears in *Extending opportunity: a national framework for study support* (DfES 1998):

> Study support is learning activity outside normal lessons which young people take part in voluntarily. Study support is, accordingly, an inclusive term, embracing many activities – with many different names and guises. Its purpose is to improve young people's motivation, build their self-esteem and help them become effective learners. Above all it aims to raise achievement.

An appealing aspect of this framework is that it can provide accreditation and be integrated with training (ITT) and continuing professional development (CPD). The document quotes a 'range of activities', of which many could be considered by the department:

- study clubs (linked to or extending curriculum subjects)

- homework clubs (facilities and support to do homework)

- space and support for coursework and exam revision

- adventurous outdoor activities (in a non-English-speaking environment)

- creative ventures (music, drama, dance, film and the full range of arts) – in a MFL or community language

- residential events – study weeks or weekends

- opportunities to pursue particular interests (Latin, Arabic, Greek, Mandarin Chinese)

- mentoring by adults or other pupils

- learning about learning (thinking skills, accelerated learning)

- community activities (environmental work).

(Adapted from *Study Support in Teacher Training and Professional Development* DfES 0492/2001)

A very positive feature of this development is that those involved in the activities have a chance to experiment, free from the restricting effects of the national curriculum.

New understanding about the nature of intelligence and learning, and contemporary information about the way the brain works, have stimulated fresh approaches to learning, especially outside the classroom. Study support has been a test bed for new ideas and an opportunity for schools to identify and respond more specifically to the needs of individual pupils.

(DfES 0492/2001)

As more schools offer extended services, MFL departments could consider ways of contributing to their school's or cluster's programme that will in turn support their class work. Short early-evening courses or weekend sessions for families or parent-child activities centred on languages such as 'preparing to receive your French/German exchange pupil'; or 'preparing for your family walking/cycling/camping trip abroad' could work within certain communities. Where a school offers a four-week 'Brush up your holiday languages (Greek, Spanish, Italian, Japanese)' course, it can attract not only parents, teachers of other subjects, local businesspeople – but also some of its more able pupils. It is a good idea to start with a small, imaginative and enjoyable project, to generate interest and success.

Many schools have found study support relatively easy to set up, but more difficult to link to classroom work and to evaluate. Funding is more likely to be forthcoming where the department can show measurable outcomes: therefore, while the project is being set up, staff should think about what it might achieve at classroom level. An example of good outcomes might be improved group-work skills, more creative use of language, greater confidence in giving oral presentations, greater cultural awareness.

See Chapter 6 for more discussion of out-of-school opportunities for able pupils.

Mentors – who are they and what is their role?

The use of mentors is opening up new and exciting opportunities. There will be many successful ways of setting up mentoring and the department should be on the lookout for inspirational ideas which could fit its particular needs and culture. Initially, the school policy will decide on the focus of mentoring: some schools target underachievement or behavioural problems; others look at pupils from disadvantaged backgrounds, including those whose first language is not English. The school will also work out guidelines for mentoring, deciding on, for example, the frequency of meetings. It is important to stress that it is the relationship that matters: meetings need only be brief.

There are many possible candidates and ways of managing these roles. The LA can advertise for mentors, who may come from a community's rich population of intelligent people with time on their hands. (A retired airline pilot is a recent example.) The school may conduct a survey of community resources, by asking its staff, pupils, parents/carers to help it identify useful contacts, volunteers and their interests. The school may also write a description of a person with particular interests or qualities to suit a specific pupil.

In the MFL department, staff should consider such support for their more able pupils who

- are materially disadvantaged

- are isolated

- have English as a second language (though these pupils often achieve well in MFL classes, they may not be considering going to university)

- have unsupportive family backgrounds or many responsibilities in their home

or

- are so far ahead of their peers that they need special provision.

A nearby university may have a considerable number of foreign university students, studying for degrees in this country, and keen to have local contacts, experience of the education system and of leadership, as well as part-time work. The MFL department is in a good position to liaise with the school coordinator on matching individual mentors with pupils with special talents (the linguistically able or less able) with, say, French, Spanish, German, Italian, Japanese-speaking students on courses such as music, sport sciences, performing arts, fine art and design.

Older pupils can act as mentors to younger ones. In some schools, sixth form MFL students provide in-class support to Year 10 and 11 pupils. Sometimes, a very able senior pupil supports an able but isolated lower school pupil using a 'buddy' system.

In some cases, a specific teacher is chosen by a pupil to be their mentor for 'moral support' or emotional support.

Generally there are two types of mentoring, but these are not always clear-cut roles:

- learning mentors – who support underachieving able pupils, or help pupils to extend their work

- academic mentors – who support high achievers who are far in advance of their peers in specific disciplines. In languages, a pupil may benefit from having contact with university staff who teach such subjects as Greek, Latin, Arabic and Russian. As part of the EiC project, academic mentors held 20-minute meetings with pupils and talked about their own research and work interests. They discussed pupils' extension work and helped decide on 'action points' which were then shared with subject teachers.

Case study: an exceptionally gifted and talented pupil

Chloe (Year 10)

Chloe excels in the classroom, on the sports field, on the stage, in music activities and socially. She is a natural leader, is often elected form captain, and is well liked by her peers and her teachers. When she is asked about the future and possible careers, she throws up her hands and laughs because she simply has too many options.

She has always produced high quality homework but recently standards have begun to slip. Her evenings and weekends are filled with activity – flute lessons, netball or tennis matches, Duke of Edinburgh Award Scheme and rehearsals for plays. Chloe is becoming interested in politics too and has begun to spend hours after school sitting on a wall hotly debating topical issues with some older boys. She has asked her parents if she can go to some political meetings.

Chloe's parents are quietly concerned. They know that their daughter has a voracious appetite for learning and activity of one sort or another, but they believe that the time has come for her to choose some and give up others. Her parents also believe that teachers need to be more sensitive to the pressures they place on Chloe. She is everyone's safe A* and teachers become alarmed when they see her backsliding.

Strategies

- Bear in mind that for adolescents, 'social and emotional considerations are paramount' (George 1997: 9). Try to resolve problems over clashing commitments without pressuring Chloe. A learning mentor or a member of the pastoral team might negotiate on Chloe's behalf. Make sure she is using good time management strategies, because she will need these. She and her parents need to be aware that although she has a lot of options, having too much choice is in itself stressful.

- Work with Chloe and her parents to draw up a list of activities in which she will take a leading part and others that need to be put on hold for a while.

- Monitor her closely and alert others if she continues to take on too many activities or doesn't appear to be coping well.

Example project

Rather than set specific tasks, discuss how to double up on some of her commitments and interests. Look ahead and help her to appreciate the opportunities that her MFL competence can open up in the long term. Make sure she is focused over her MFL writing coursework and understands how to go for quality not quantity. At the same time she can practise her reading and listening skills in the MFL to develop some more complex ideas for her oral examination.

She can use her MFL reading skills to explore her favourite topics, for example music, politics/economics, current affairs, using online newspapers. If she is interested in taking a course in politics at university, contact a university department and get a suggested reading list.

The large *Collins Robert French Dictionary* (which should be in the school library!) has a very useful section with phrases that are commonly used in outlining written discussion. Using some of these as models would help her develop her debating skills in both French and English, as they can be applied to a range of political topics.

A similar section also appears in other languages in large Collins dictionaries.

The school library/resource and learning centre

Departments should try to build up the resources each year, with a variety of media. Liaise with the librarian to ensure MFL gets a fair share of the budget for more able pupils and acquires a range of suitable material.

Publicise the MFL section to pupils and take groups there to explore and practise so they will venture in on their own. For example, a carousel of 3–4 activities, using listening stations, a website visit and one sedentary, easy-to-manage activity such as a quiz or crossword, once organised, can be replicated until the entire year group has been introduced to the library and the librarian.

Here are some suggestions for building up the MFL section:

- Print media.

- FLAs and exchange schools are a good source. A keen contact abroad can organise a suitable collection for adolescents, of used magazines, reading books, song books, which can be swapped for similar material in English. The collection should include literature in the target language, short stories, short novels, poetry, plays.

- Some schools stock a range of MFL magazines – not just on current events, but also teen magazines such as *Sugar* in German; they also have a whole range of newspapers archived in several languages.

- Fairy tales – for able pupils to summarise or retell for younger pupils – also work well.

- Look for books with good clear illustrations such as Dorling-Kindersley books (some are available in German and French) and HarperCollins titles.

- Dictionaries: printed and on CD.

- Listening material: CDs and/or tapes with tapescripts.

- Computers with online access.

- Reading material on CDs.

- Games, such as Mille Bornes in French, Trivial Pursuit in German, Monopoly in Spanish.

- Outside sources: some pupils have an insatiable need for more resources. They may be able to use a local university, YG&T or other agencies.

- List suitable MFL resources and links to helpful websites on the school website. Pupils can help to keep the department's list of sites up to date and log their 'top tips' for good sites.

Links with parents/carers

Departments could work with parents/carers to develop a booklet or evening session on how to support their able and talented children. Parents of such children sometimes put them through repetitive exam-practice tests (using commercial resources) in the belief that it will help them, when they could do interesting projects such as watch a foreign film, try cooking Italian/French/Spanish recipes, or go to the art gallery instead.

Wherever possible, keep parents informed of the opportunities available outside school time; encourage them to share their expertise, information and ideas for supporting their children in your subject, with the department and with other parents/carers. Schools that have at first been wary of pressure from parents have found that good communication brought positive results, as parents had more idea of how best to help. Some parents have set up their own support groups and have continued to work with gifted children even after their own children have left school.

Liaising with external agencies

When pupils are taking part in externally run programmes, such as a youth orchestra or an athletics team, the department needs to be aware of these commitments and the important dates associated with them. In this way, able linguists can be helped to phase their work so that they are not under pressure from conflicting and unreasonable demands. There are relatively few fixed dates for GCSE and a few minutes spent looking at the calendar and strategising over coursework, oral examinations and so on will relieve undue stress for pupil and teacher.

Summary

- Departments need to work with the strengths of linguistically able pupils with special educational needs.

- Liaise with the SENCO on good strategies for individual pupils.

- Work at integrating the contribution of teaching assistants.

- Foreign language assistants can be used flexibly to support more able pupils.

- The study support scheme has great potential for imaginative projects that will enrich the curriculum.

- Mentoring of individual pupils can help, on a short-term or long-term basis.

- Work with the school library to build up resources and make good use of them.

- Keep parents/carers in the picture.

- Liaise with external agencies to ease conflicting demands on able pupils.

CHAPTER 6

Beyond the classroom

- Visits
- Residentials
- Competitions and language festivals
- Summer schools
- Masterclasses
- Links with universities, business and other organisations
- Distance learning
- Experts
- Endnote

The purpose of this chapter is to look at some of the opportunities available to the more able MFL learner outside the classroom, and some of the resources outside the classroom that the MFL teacher can make use of.

For the MFL teacher, many of the ways of working outside the classroom are invaluable because of the nature of the subject. They allow for real or realistic experience of a 'foreign' culture: extensive sessions where pupils can move quickly through a variety of activities and increase their confidence as well as see the benefits of being even more competent. There are many exciting initiatives from which teachers can get inspiration to develop projects which fit their particular school and community. Imagination, energy, contacts and time are all (!) you need.

Visits

Even without going abroad, pupils can have an authentic sample of another culture and language.

- One class studying Japanese visits the Japanese Embassy, where they are able to see a slide show on Japan, try on traditional Japanese clothes, try calligraphy and origami. The programme, run by the Education Officer, is called Club taishikan (Embassy).

- In England, two teachers of French working in different schools set up penfriend links between their pupils. They found that their pupils were keen to send e-mails in French to others who were at a similar level of competence. The teachers arranged a languages-based afternoon at one of the schools so that the penfriends could meet. A low-budget but very motivating visit!

- A visit to an art gallery, with help from their education staff, could centre on works by Spanish, Italian, French, Belgian or German artists and be delivered in the relevant language.

- Theatre trips to see works in translation are another way of experiencing another culture.

Since a lot of teacher effort can go into trips, staff should consider in advance how they might monitor the way such outings contribute to enriching pupils' learning and understanding. A report on the effectiveness of the introduction of the Gifted and Talented strand within Excellence in Cities during 1999–2000 made the points that, although target setting

> is a valuable tool in raising standards and the quality of provision . . . more thought needs to be given to the range of targets and to the success criteria; the number of out of school visits completed by a school is not a valuable criterion of success; the ultimate success criteria should focus on producing creative thinkers rather than training pupils to pass exams.
>
> (www.standards.dfes.gov.uk/giftedandtalented/goodpractice/Publications/
> nordangliaresearchproject/summary/)

Therefore, it makes sense to look for ways of challenging pupils to evaluate their outings – how might it have changed or confirmed their beliefs about another culture? Could they produce, say, an imaginary interview in the TL with a painter, asking about her/his choice of colours, subjects, or imagine what headings that painter might have used on her/his website?

Residentials

Trips abroad

As anyone who has organised and/or led a trip abroad knows, these involve an enormous amount of work. These days, teachers leading trips abroad also need to be aware of the LA risk assessment policy and to carry out a risk assessment. Lines of communication and responsibility need to be very clear. Especially with exchanges, if a pupil has cause to be unhappy, he needs to be able to get that message through to the organisers at any time. Back-up from foreign staff must be ensured. It also remains to be seen how MFL teachers will be able to accompany trips in school time.

Having mentioned some of the obstacles, it is motivating for teachers to know that the benefits of such visits – particularly exchanges – are often life-changing in the long term. Parents/carers are sometimes surprisingly willing to make financial sacrifices in order to give their children an opportunity they may not have had themselves.

If there is no possibility for a school to run a trip abroad, there are organisations that will do the work of matching individual pupils with host families. The British Council, for example, offers bursaries to 14–18 year olds who are studying German to take part in subsidised two-week courses. Pupils live with host families, go on excursions and attend classes. Alternatively, students in England can win a fellowship to attend a German school for two weeks during which they work on an individual research project. They need to have a good level of German and be over 16 at the time of the visit.

Some other opportunities offered by the British Council are:

- for pupils (from age 13) in the former ILEA boroughs attending state secondary schools and colleges, there is funding available for exchanges through the Lefèvre trust. See www.britishcouncil.org/schoolpartnerships-france-lefevre-trust.htm.

- setting up links with partner schools in several countries (including Japan and Russia) for online projects.

- a Chinese language immersion course for teachers and students.

The MFL department can also team up with another department. For example, a rafting or skiing trip to France or Germany can be organised to have a language element. One very successful trip to Paris combined the expertise of the art, history and MFL departments and enriched the experience of staff as well as students.

Residentials in the UK

Kilve Court, Somerset runs residential courses for gifted and talented children, including MFL courses: www.kilvecourt.org.

Competitions and language festivals

The beauty of competitions is that they can particularly appeal to very able pupils – who will often decide themselves to 'have a go'. For some pupils, it may be sufficient just to advertise the competition. According to Joan Freeman:

> Although at first glance competitions appear to be passive in only tapping what is already there, in fact they are active in eliciting, stimulating and challenging

talents in many different fields. Because they can activate and strengthen the feeling for the subject matter, they improve knowledge and skills. Struggling with the tasks of the competition enhances the abilities to work autonomously, while researching, experimenting, problem solving, persevering.

(Freeman 2002: 21)

Having said this, Freeman goes on to state that on the whole competitions appeal rather more to boys than girls.

In England, there is no Languages equivalent of the BBC Young Musician of the Year competition or the Federal Language Contest held in Germany. There are a few opportunities, however:

- The TES Newsday is a one-day cross-curricular competition to produce a newspaper. It can be produced in a foreign language or in English. Information is on www.newsday.co.uk.

- Language festivals (usually organised by the LA), where language activities are offered throughout a day, give pupils insight into different writing systems and grammatical systems. For example, one LA organised a Languages Festival Day, with competitions for Year 8 pupils, tasters of different languages and a MFL performance with a Theatre in Education company.

- The British Council runs a Chinese Speaking Competition, with a prize of a trip to China, for pupils from Years 7 to 13 studying Chinese in England.

- CILT organised a European Languages Day as part of a Europe-wide project. CILT is also a source of information on the European Award for Languages which rewards various creative and imaginative projects, including some from secondary schools. Some projects involve use of British Sign Language and Community languages. www.cilt.org.uk.

Summer schools

Summer schools are an import from abroad: for example, North America, where there is a long tradition of summer camps. In the US, academic summer schools have been used to boost the achievement of pupils in schools where standards are low compared with those in the UK. When NAGTY first organised a UK version, their model was the Johns Hopkins Centre for Talented Youth (CTY) summer school. There were obvious benefits for the pupils who attended, but not all the outcomes were foreseen. According to Sloan (Head of the Student Academy, which ran the summer school) and Frost:

Academically and socially the Summer School experience has already proved to be life-changing for all who have taken part.

The curious by-product has been the innovative way in which the role of the classroom teacher (as applied subject academics) on Summer School has developed to also be simultaneously a mediator and a beneficiary of the subject expertise being given by the university academic. This highly effective mode of CPD is one which clearly has legs . . .

(Sloan and Frost 2004)

LAs also run summer schools lasting up to ten days, particularly for Year 6 to Year 9 pupils. One language-based summer school was built around a day trip to France. Unfortunately, specific DfES funding to LAs for these summer schools stopped in 2005.

Feedback from pupils who have attended these summer schools suggest that they could benefit most children, not just the gifted and talented. A quotation from Freeman gives this interesting point of view:

> . . . often reported social benefits do not prove the value of the courses. Other courses or holidays in mixed-ability groups enjoying time together could have as beneficial social effects, not least in enabling the labelled gifted to mingle with normal children. Indeed, the effects of different types of social contexts on gifted children have never been investigated. At root, there also seems to be the supposition that the gifted are emotionally more fragile and need special social contexts such as gifted summer schools to feel good about themselves. Yet evidence of greater than usual emotional fragility among the gifted is more than doubtful.
>
> (Freeman 1997 quoted in Freeman 2002: 43–44)

Other courses abroad, via an independent agency, can be found through InTuition Languages Ltd, which advertises its 'independent service for those looking for a suitable overseas language course'. Accommodation can also be arranged. Overseas courses in a range of languages are listed on www.in-languages.com.

Masterclasses

Some of these were run within Excellence in Cities consortiums. They could involve pupils working at different levels, focusing on particular topics, such as grammar. They could also be cross-curricular, combining two or more subject areas, but delivered in a MFL.

The most successful models seem to be where lecturers in a subject in Higher Education deliver workshops with teachers and their pupils. Teachers are able to enhance their skills and collaborate on projects, to their own and their pupils' benefit. Pupils have first-hand experience of working with someone who teaches at higher education level.

Links with universities, business and other organisations

Some universities abroad – for example, in Canada – are developing Advanced Placement schemes so that exceptional pupils can work towards university accreditation while still at school. This has the advantage of allowing pupils to stay with their social group while having access to challenging work. More information is available at www.ap.ca.

As part of a Young Applicants in Schools Scheme (YASS), the Open University offers several MFL courses: www.open.ac.uk/yass.

Oxbridge Academic Programs has a French prep experience for US students in Grades 8 and 9 which is open to UK pupils, for a fee: www.oxbridgeprograms.com.

The International Baccalaureate, which is also gaining popularity, is another vehicle for setting up a pathway for exceptional Key Stage 4 pupils: www.ibo.org.

Distance learning

Vektor has been running tutor-supported distance learning at A Level in French, German and Spanish since 1998: details are on the Vektor website: www.vektor.com.

The BBC has begun to offer free courses, for example stand-alone courses in Spanish and French. Other content ranges over several languages, from beginners to advanced level. These would make a good starting point for short 'taster' courses in languages that are rarely offered in schools. The BBC also offer topical news updates in French and Spanish. See their website at www.bbc.co.uk/languages.

Some businesses and firms show a lively interest in modern languages but links to able pupils are rare. However, more companies are becoming aware of the value of investing in the community and are encouraging their employees to make a contribution in schools in roles such as mentoring.

There is at least one example of a school that offers translation services in community languages to local firms. Some schools persuade local businesses to sponsor 'programmes' for gifted and talented pupils either with funding or resources/equipment. In Key Stage 4, work experience can be arranged through links with businesses in other countries.

Experts

Suitable tutors from universities, languages colleges, the world of business – with consultation with the school, consortium or LA – can be invited to work with gifted linguists. Former pupils of the school who have made their careers in languages (or with the help of languages) are good role models for pupils and are often willing to visit their old school.

Other opportunities can be explored on the Standards website: www.standards.dfes.gov.uk/giftedandtalented.

Endnote

All this activity adds up to a rich menu of possibilities for the able pupil. It remains to be seen just how many such projects are sustainable beyond the short term. Perhaps the way forward for the UK, which is just beginning to look at creative ways of providing for more able pupils outside school hours, is to consider what Freeman (1998) calls 'The Sports Approach: identification by provision'.

Because there is little research evidence on the long-term benefits of out-of-school provision, she recommends an alternative to the (US) model of selecting pupils on the basis of certain qualities for a specific course.

Freeman has proposed that given the opportunity, and with some guidance, the talented (and motivated) should be able to select themselves to work at any subject at a more advanced and broader level – the 'Sports Approach'. In the same way as those who are talented and motivated can select themselves for extra tuition and practice in sports, they could opt for extra foreign languages or physics. This would mean, of course, that such facilities must be available to all, as sport is, rather than only to those pre-selected by tests, experts, supportive homes or money to pay for extras. This is neither an expensive route, nor does it risk emotional disturbance to the children by removing them from the company of their friends. It makes use of research-based understanding of the very able, notably the benefit of focusing on a defined area of the pupil's interest, as well as providing each one with the facilities they need to learn with and make progress.

The pupil makes some form of commitment to participation in the extra education, but loses that opportunity if the commitment is not sustained. The Sports Approach model is used in Somerset.

Summary

- Visits, in addition to their social aspect, can provide valuable enrichment for more able children.

- Visits abroad, provided they are well organised, can be the most educationally rewarding of experiences for talented linguists.

- More able pupils, their parents/carers and teachers should be on the lookout for competitions that inspire and motivate.

- Summer schools are offering a wide choice of study opportunities that are inspiring and fun for participants.

- Masterclasses where schoolteachers learn along with their pupils are highly motivating to all concerned.

- Good links with universities, business and other organisations can be mutually profitable and give able pupils inspiration for their future role.

- Contacts with experts are another means of raising aspirations for more able and underachieving pupils.

Appendices

Institutional quality standards in gifted and talented education

A – Effective teaching and learning strategies

Generic Elements	Entry	Developing	Exemplary
1. Identification	i. The school/college has learning conditions and systems to identify gifted and talented pupils in all year groups and an agreed definition and shared understanding of the meaning of 'gifted and talented' within its own, local and national contexts.	i. Individual pupils are screened annually against clear criteria at school/college and subject/topic level.	i. **Multiple criteria and sources of evidence** are used to identify gifts and talents, including through the use of a broad range of quantitative and qualitative data.
	ii. An **accurate record** of the identified gifted and talented population is kept and updated.	ii. The record is used to identify under-achievement and **exceptional achievement** (both within and outside the population) and to track/review pupil **progress.**	ii. The record is supported by a comprehensive monitoring, progress planning and reporting system which all staff regularly share and contribute to.
	iii. The identified gifted and talented population broadly reflects the school/college's **social and economic composition,** gender and ethnicity.	iii. **Identification** systems address issues of **multiple exceptionality** (pupils with specific gifts/talents and special educational needs).	iii. Identification processes are regularly reviewed and refreshed in the light of pupil performance and value-added data. The gifted and talented population is fully representative of the school/college's population.
Evidence			
Next steps			
2. Effective provision in the classroom	i. The school/college addresses the different needs of the gifted and talented population by providing a stimulating learning environment and by extending the teaching repertoire.	i. Teaching and learning strategies are diverse and flexible, meeting the needs of distinct pupil groups within the gifted and talented population (e.g. able underachievers, exceptionally able).	i. The school/college has established a range of methods to find out what works best in the classroom, and shares this within the school/college and with other schools and colleges.
	ii. Teaching and learning is differentiated and delivered through both individual and group activities.	ii. A range of challenging learning and teaching strategies is evident in lesson planning and delivery. **Independent learning** skills are developed.	ii. Teaching and learning are suitably challenging and varied, incorporating the breadth, depth and pace required to progress high achievement. Pupils routinely work independently and self-reliantly.

	Column 1	Column 2
	iii. Opportunities exist to extend learning through **new technologies**.	iii. The use of **new technologies** across the curriculum is focused on **personalised learning** needs.	iii. The innovative use of new technologies raises the achievement and motivation of gifted and talented pupils.
Evidence			
Next steps			
3. Standards	i. Levels of **attainment** and **achievement** for gifted and talented pupils are comparatively high in relation to the rest of the school/college population and are in line with those of similar pupils in similar schools/colleges.	i. Levels of **attainment** and **achievement** for gifted and talented pupils are broadly consistent across the gifted and talented population and above those of similar pupils in similar schools/colleges.	i. Levels of attainment and achievement for gifted and talented pupils indicate sustainability over time and are well above those of similar pupils in similar schools/colleges.
	ii. Self-evaluation indicates that gifted and talented provision is satisfactory.	ii. Self-evaluation indicates that gifted and talented provision is good.	ii. Self-evaluation indicates that gifted and talented provision is very good or excellent.
	iii. Schools/colleges' gifted and talented education programmes are explicitly linked to the achievement of SMART outcomes and these highlight improvements in pupils' attainment and achievement.		
Evidence			
Next steps			

B – Enabling curriculum entitlement and choice

	Column 1	Column 2
4. Enabling curriculum entitlement and choice	i. Curriculum organisation is flexible, with opportunities for enrichment and increasing subject/topic choice. Pupils are provided with support and guidance in making choices.	i. The curriculum offers opportunities and guidance to pupils which enable them to work beyond their age and/or phase, and across subjects or topics, according to their aptitudes and interests.	i. The curriculum offers personalised learning pathways for pupils which maximise individual potential, retain flexibility of future choices, extend well beyond test/examination requirements and result in sustained impact on pupil attainment and achievement.
Evidence			
Next steps			

Definitions for words and phrases in bold are provided in the glossary in the Quality Standards *User Guide*, available at www2.teachernet.gov.uk/gat. QS Model October 2005

© Crown Copyright 2005–2007.

Generic Elements	Entry	Developing	Exemplary
5. Assessment for learning	i. Processes of data analysis and pupil assessment are employed throughout the school/college to plan learning for gifted and talented pupils.	i. Routine progress reviews, using both qualitative and quantitative data, make effective use of prior, predictive and value-added attainment data to plan for progression in pupils' learning.	i. Assessment data are used by teachers and across the school/college to ensure challenge and sustained progression in individual pupils' learning.
	ii. Dialogue with pupils provides focused feedback which is used to plan future learning.	ii. Systematic oral and written feedback helps pupils to set challenging curricular targets.	ii. Formative assessment and individual target setting combine to maximise and celebrate pupils' achievements.
	iii. Self and peer assessment, based on clear understanding of criteria, are used to increase pupils' responsibility for learning.	iii. Pupils reflect on their own skill development and are involved in the design of their own targets and tasks.	iii. Classroom practice regularly requires pupils to reflect on their own progress against targets, and engage in the direction of their own learning.
Evidence			
Next steps			
6. Transfer and transition	i. Shared processes, using agreed criteria, are in place to ensure the productive transfer of information from one setting to another (i.e. from class to class, year to year and school/college to school/college).	i. Transfer information concerning gifted and talented pupils, including parental input, informs targets for pupils to ensure progress in learning. Particular attention is given to including new admissions.	i. Transfer data concerning gifted and talented pupils are used to inform planning of teaching and learning at subject/aspect/topic and individual pupil level, and to ensure progression according to ability rather than age or phase.
Evidence			
Next steps			

D – School/college organisation

Generic Elements	Entry	Developing	Exemplary
7. Leadership	i. A named member of the governing body, senior management team and the lead professional responsible for gifted and talented education have clearly directed responsibilities for motivating and driving gifted and talented provision. The head teacher actively champions gifted and talented provision.	i. Responsibility for gifted and talented provision is distributed, and evaluation of its impact shared, at all levels in the school/college. Staff subscribe to policy at all levels. Governors play a significant supportive and evaluative role.	i. Organisational structures, communication channels and the deployment of staff (e.g. workforce remodelling) are flexible and creative in supporting the delivery of personalised learning. Governors take a lead in celebrating achievements of gifted and talented pupils.
Evidence			
Next steps			

8. Policy	i. The gifted and talented policy is integral to the school/college's inclusion agenda and approach to personalised learning, feeds into and from the single school/college improvement plan and is consistent with other policies.	i. The policy directs and reflects best practice in the school/college, is regularly reviewed and is clearly linked to other policy documentation.	i. The policy includes input from the whole-school/college community and is regularly refreshed in the light of innovative national and international practice.
Evidence			
Next steps			
9. School/college ethos and pastoral care	i. The school/college sets high expectations, recognises achievement and celebrates the successes of all its pupils. ii. The school/college identifies and addresses the particular social and emotional needs of gifted and talented pupils in consultation with pupils, parents and carers.	i. The school/college fosters an environment which promotes positive behaviour for learning. Pupils are listened to and their views taken into account. ii. Strategies exist to counteract bullying and any adverse effects of social and curriculum pressures. Specific support for able underachievers and pupils from different cultures and social backgrounds is available and accessible.	i. An ethos of ambition and achievement is agreed and shared by the whole school/college community. Success across a wide range of abilities is celebrated. ii. The school/college places equal emphasis on high achievement and emotional well being, underpinned by programmes of support personalised to the needs of gifted and talented pupils. There are opportunities for pupils to use their gifts to benefit other pupils and the wider community.
Evidence			
Next steps			
10. Staff development	i. Staff have received professional development in meeting the needs of gifted and talented pupils.	i. The induction programme for new staff addresses gifted and talented issues, both at whole school/college and specific subject/aspect level.	i. There is ongoing audit of staff needs and an appropriate range of professional development in gifted and talented education. Professional development is informed by research and collaboration within and beyond the school/college.

Definitions for words and phrases in bold are provided in the glossary in the Quality Standards *User Guide*, available at www2.teachernet.gov.uk/gat. QS Model October 2005

© Crown Copyright 2005–2007

Generic Elements	Entry	Developing	Exemplary
	ii. The lead professional responsible for gifted and talented education has received appropriate professional development.	ii. Subject/aspect and phase leaders have received specific professional development in meeting the needs of gifted and talented pupils.	ii. Priorities for the development of gifted and talented provision are included within a professional development entitlement for all staff and are monitored through performance management processes.
Evidence			
Next steps			
11. Resources	i. Provision for gifted and talented pupils is supported by appropriate budgets and resources.	i. Allocated resources include school/college based and nationally available resources, and these have a significant and measurable impact on the progress that pupils make and their attitudes to learning.	i. Resources are used to stimulate innovative and experimental practice, which is shared throughout the school/college and which are regularly reviewed for impact and best value.
Evidence			
Next steps			
12. Monitoring and evaluation	i. Subject and phase audits focus on the quality of teaching and learning for gifted and talented pupils. Whole school/college targets are set using prior attainment data.	i. Performance against targets (including at pupil level) is regularly reviewed. Targets include qualitative pastoral and curriculum outcomes as well as numerical data.	i. Performance against targets is rigorously evaluated against clear criteria. Qualitative and quantitative outcomes inform whole-school/college self-evaluation processes.
	ii. Elements of provision are planned against clear objectives within effective whole-school self-evaluation processes.	ii. All elements, including non-academic aspects of gifted and talented provision, are planned to clear objectives and are subjected to detailed evaluation.	ii. The school/college examines and challenges its own provision to inform development of further experimental and innovative practice in collaboration with other schools/colleges.
Evidence			
Next steps			

E – Strong partnerships beyond the school

13. Engaging with the community, families and beyond	i. Parents/carers are aware of the school's/college's policy on gifted and talented provision, contribute to its identification processes and are kept informed of developments in gifted and talented provision, including through the School Profile.	i. Progression of gifted and talented pupils is enhanced by home-school/college partnerships. There are strategies to engage and support hard-to-reach parents/carers.		i. Parents/carers are actively engaged in extending provision. Support for gifted and talented provision is integrated with other children's services (e.g. Sure Start, EAL, traveller, refugee, LAC Services).	
	ii. The school/college shares good practice and has some collaborative provision with other schools, colleges and the wider community.	ii. A coherent strategy for networking with other schools, colleges and local community organisations extends and enriches provision.		ii. There is strong emphasis on collaborative and innovative working with other schools/colleges which impacts on quality of provision locally, regionally and nationally.	
Evidence					
Next steps					
14. Learning beyond the classroom	i. There are opportunities for pupils to learn beyond the school/college day and site (extended hours and out-of-school activities).	i. A coherent programme of enrichment and extension activities (through extended hours and out-of-school activities) complements teaching and learning and helps identify pupils' latent gifts and talents.		i. Innovative models of learning beyond the classroom are developed in collaboration with local and national schools/colleges to further enhance teaching and learning.	
	ii. Pupils participate in dedicated gifted and talented activities (e.g. summer schools) and their participation is recorded.	ii. Local and national provision helps meet individual pupils' learning needs, e.g. NAGTY membership, accessing outreach, local enrichment programmes.		ii. Coherent strategies are used to direct and develop individual expert performance via external agencies, e.g. HE/FE links, online support, and local/regional/national programmes.	
Evidence					
Next steps					

Definitions for words and phrases in bold are provided in the glossary in the Quality Standards *User Guide*, available at www2.teachernet.gov.uk/gat. QS Model October 2005

© Crown Copyright 2005–2007.

MFL departmental audit of provision for the most able pupils

Stage 1

The more able cohort in MFL

If you have identified the top 5–10% (the more able or gifted and talented cohort) in each year group, look critically at the composition of that cohort to see if any groups of pupils are under-represented in MFL.

	Y7	Y8	Y9	Y10	Y11
% of pupils in each year group who receive free school meals					
% of pupils in more able cohort who receive free school meals					
% of boys in each year group					
% of boys in more able cohort in each year group					
% of girls in each year group					
% of girls in more able cohort in each year group					
% of ethnic minority pupils in each year group					
% of ethnic minority pupils in the more able cohort in each year group					

In MFL

Percentages of pupils attaining Level 4 and above

Attainment in KS3 teacher assessments:	National averages		
	Above	In line	below
% of all pupils achieving Level 4 and above was:			
% of boys achieving Level 4 and above was:			
% of girls achieving Level 4 and above was:			

Take-up of MFL at GCSE and post-16

Language	% of pupils taking language at KS4	% boys taking language at KS4	% girls taking language at KS4

	% of pupils taking language post-16	% boys taking language post-16	% girls taking language post-16

In general, how do the most able pupils react to each language?

a) Enthusiastic _____

b) Non-committal _____

c) Disengaged _____

If b or c, can you pinpoint why?

Extracurricular

What extracurricular support/activities are provided for the most able in each year group? (Include clubs, masterclasses, extension classes, visits, invited experts, links with business/colleges, etc.)

	Extracurricular Support/Activity
Year 7	
Year 8	
Year 9	
Year 10	
Year 11	

Appendix 2.1

General

	Yes/No/ In progress	Priority for action?
1. Has the department developed a policy on its provision for the more able?		
2. Does it have a more able/G&T coordinator or representative who liaises directly with the school more able/G&T coordinator?		
3. Are the most able students clearly identified in subject registers?		

Stage 2

Highlight all areas where achievement or provision in your department is lacking.

Decide on about 3 priorities to raise standards or improve provision for your most able and draw up an action plan making it clear:

- What your success criteria are or what you hope to achieve

- What action will be taken

- When the action will be taken and by whom

- Where you will go for help

- What resources you need

- How you will monitor your progress

- What your deadline is for assessing your success.

From *Meeting the Needs of Your Most Able Pupils: Modern Foreign Languages*, Routledge 2008

Departmental action plan for improving provision for the most able

Priority	Success criteria	Actions	When?	By whom?	Resources/Support agencies
1.					
					Review Date
2.					
					Review Date
3.					
					Review Date

From *Meeting the Needs of Your Most Able Pupils: Modern Foreign Languages*, Routledge 2008

Appendix 2.2

Acceleration checklist

Before accelerating a child, have you:	Yes/No
1. Explored all available strategies for providing for that child within his/her peer group?	
2. Consulted fully with: Parents *(Such consultation should include advice on pros and cons of acceleration and time for parents to consider this information)* Teachers The child *(Children are rarely consulted or involved in the process)* Any receiving schools or colleges *(Are they prepared to accept young pupils? Can they provide appropriate programmes of study for them?)*	
3. Considered: The emotional/social maturity of the child? The physical maturity of the child? Areas of weakness within curriculum (e.g. presentation skills or spelling)? The friendship ties of the child? The long-term impact on the child? *(e.g. There can be conflict at adolescence between parents and children when children want to socialise with and behave like their classmates and not their chronological age group. Is the child likely to benefit from going to university early?)*	
4. Drawn up a short-term plan with all concerned parties for the pupil's educational provision?	
5. Made arrangements for regular review of the pupil's progress throughout his/her schooling?	
6. Told parents/carers, child and teachers of agencies that can support them if there are difficulties? *(E.g. NAGC Youth Agency)*	

 From *Meeting the Needs of Your Most Able Pupils: Modern Foreign Languages*, Routledge 2008

> ## Planning for challenge: a worked example based on Year 8 Unit 11 topic *A la mode*

Context

This is not a lesson, but an example of a way through a topic where more able pupils make decisions about the vocabulary they will need. The teacher can avoid micro-marking and support pupils as they put together the language they will need to perform well on an end-of-unit assessment. It could be used with a top set or, within a mixed ability class, with a group of more able pupils.

Essential prior learning

Pupils should:

- know colour words
- have an understanding of regular adjective agreement and position
- know the names of a variety of countries and nationalities
- have begun to use the perfect tense of some common verbs
- know the names of parts of the body.

The medium-term plan for the topic would look something like this:

- map the topic
- divide up the task of researching the language needed for the unit assessment
- practise using colour words in sentences
- looking at/revisiting language for preferences
- reading practice using a website or prepared examples or passages from a textbook
- building more detailed descriptions
- revising parts of the body, hair styles, eye colour (etc.) to reuse within this topic
- giving reasons
- discussing prices (using comparatives)
- listening practice prepared by the FLA from pupils' lists
- setting up the classroom organisation for the end-of-unit assessment (an extended role-play); discussion of marking criteria (with all the group being trained to assess)

- more input of language structures found to be necessary to build more complex sentences

- practice of role-plays

- presentation of role-plays

- feedback: the teacher monitors and picks up on the needs of pupils, models language to the whole group or small groups as necessary.

Although the scheme of work suggests using French catalogues (*La Redoute* is a possibility), it is very noticeable that much of the vocabulary to do with current fashion is English-based. This makes comprehension easy but does not provide such good material for making grammar points. However, it is worth using such vocabulary to practise reading the 'borrowed' words, while considering how differently they are pronounced in French (or another TL).

Beginning the topic

1. Begin by getting pupils to produce a mind map of the topic with some of the nouns and adjectives they would want to use to discuss clothing and fashion. If it is not possible for them to produce a mind map in French, they could be allowed a short window of English talk-time to draw up a want list, research the vocabulary – and redraw the map later in French.

2. Pupils could divide their 'want' list between them and look up vocabulary in an English-French dictionary, paying attention to getting the gender correct.

3. Pupils feed back their results. Lists are collected and typed up for distribution in the next lesson. At this point the teacher can monitor dictionary use and correct any misunderstandings (assessing for learning).

4. Pupils can produce their own mind map, this time in French.

5. Pupils can use highlighters to divide vocabulary into easy/difficult and set themselves learning targets. Their partners will test them, say, with an immediate test and one in the following lesson. By giving themselves a few minutes to look at the list and then testing each other on the easy words, they can focus on the more difficult ones for a test in a later lesson.

6. Extra activity, if needed: the teacher can model and pupils copy sentences using colour adjectives and possessive adjectives, working their way around their mind map with a partner:

   Décris tes baskets préférés . . .
   Mes baskets préférés sont blancs.
   Mon t-shirt préféré est noir.
   Mon blouson préféré est orange et noir.
   Mon short préféré est beige.

Year 8 Unit 11 topic *A la mode* – example of one lesson within this sequence: demonstrative adjectives

Starter activity

Using demonstrative adjectives (*ce/cet/cette/ces*). Saying this/that in French.

Instructions: *Groupez ces cartes. C'est à vous de décider le nombre de groupes, et de justifier votre décision.* (5 minutes)

Comparez vos résultats avec votre partenaire. Vous êtes d'accord, oui ou non? Si oui, faites les changements nécessaires.

ces Anglaises	cet Espagnol
cette Mexicaine	cette Algérienne
ces Suédois	cet Africain
ce Norvégien	ces Africaines
cet Allemand	ces Indiennes
cet Haïtien	ce Québécois
ces Québécoises	ce Mexicain

Instead of using clothes, this example uses nationalities. If you can think of any clothes beginning with 'h', you could keep to the topic! However, using easily recognised nouns makes it easier to focus more on the form of the adjective and allow pupils to try to find underlying patterns. To link the nationalities with clothes, an artistic member of the group could produce an illustrated diagram (on an OHT, as a large poster for the classroom wall or for display on an interactive whiteboard) on a multicultural theme:

Cet Indien porte un turban.
Cette Mexicaine porte un grand chapeau.
Cet Africain porte un . . .

Notes to accompany the starter activity

The idea of this lesson (or lesson within a lesson) is to allow more able pupils to use the higher order skill of deduction to discover and explain a certain pattern.

Possible scaffolding:

- Provide (4-column) grid to fill in, or partly filled in.

- Use IT software to create a version of the exercise so that pupils get immediate feedback.

Pupils attempt this on their own, then compare their results with a partner. The pair then compare their results with another pair. All groups provide feedback to a larger group, attempting to justify their decisions. Towards the end of the lesson, a pupil or group of pupils will recap the rules for using demonstrative adjectives and take questions from the others. The teacher will elicit – if the pupils do not mention it at that point – the central importance of the gender of nouns. In the bigger picture, the pattern the pupils 'discover' is repeated with similar adjectives not only in French, but across a whole group of languages.

Pupils may decide to group the words according to their meaning and geographical area. This is, of course, a valid solution. If all the pupils do this, then the teacher can ask: what would happen if you ignored the meaning (i.e. looked only at the form)?

Further questions:

Teacher asks, in TL:

'If you used *le, l', la, les* as column headings, would you have to change anything else?'

'Can you predict what would happen if you wanted to add an adjective to this phrase?'

For example:

petit/e/s

Solution:

ce petit Indien

ces petits Anglais

but

ce petit Africain (not cet)

This would make the point that the *cet* form is about sound – it's harder to say *ce Africain* than *cet Africain*. Pupils can practise the word pairs paying attention to the way that the final consonant of one word is pronounced when the next word begins with a vowel (or silent 'h'). The teacher should try to get the pupils to work this 'rule' out for themselves by listening to the teacher or FLA. Also, it is important to encourage slower accurate delivery, rather than the opposite. Speed can come later!

This set of words is good not only for grammatical purposes, but also to look at and practise other sounds. For example:

- differences between the sounds in English and French. Norway – *Norvège* because 'w' does not occur in French in words of Latin origin. In words borrowed from other languages, for example *wagon*, 'w' is usually converted to the (voiced) sound 'v'.

- *Haïti* – can they think of any words in English that have a diaeresis? What is its function? How would the word be pronounced without it? Can they use their dictionaries to find out any differences in pronunciation between *Haïti* and *Haïtien*?

An extension activity would be to research some more nationalities or examples of words using *ce/cet/cette/ces* and make up a rap:

cet Indien, ce Mexicain, cet Haïtien, cet Algérien . . .

Questioning for differentiation

- The teacher should watch for an opportunity to ask: if *ce/cet/cette/ces* mean both this and that, how do you say 'this sweater or that sweater?' Pupils try finding the solution in the dictionary.

- Further extension: The teacher watches for pupils who can move on to give reasons using *parce que/parce qu'il est/elles sont* . . . and a range of adjectives:

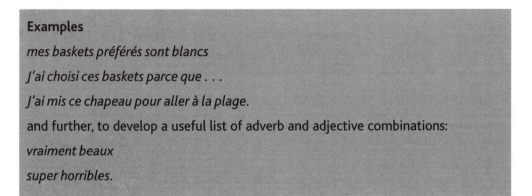

Examples

mes baskets préférés sont blancs

J'ai choisi ces baskets parce que . . .

J'ai mis ce chapeau pour aller à la plage.

and further, to develop a useful list of adverb and adjective combinations:

vraiment beaux

super horribles.

Here, the teacher models emphatic delivery of adjectives and adverb-adjective combinations, with syllables separated, as in: ri-di-cule! These can be used to great effect in the assessment.

Setting up the group for assessment

There is an argument for alternating between assessing individuals within a group and assessing a group as a whole. If all the members of the group get the same mark, the onus is on the stronger members to bring the others' performances up. It is also easier for the audience to act as assessors and award marks to the group rather than to individuals.

The teacher can discuss assessment criteria with the class/group. These can be a combination of the linguistic features – authentic accent and accuracy – and the dramatic ones – clarity, audibility, interest – plus a further mark for balanced contributions, to encourage all members to perform roughly the same amount.

Pupils can assess each others' performances after each role-play, when they will have a pause for reflection and making notes on points they have noticed. The teacher should also award marks and make notes. Pupils can be surprisingly fair, but the teacher may have to provide a counterbalance if pupils are biased in favour of their friends! If pupils need more incentive to listen carefully to others' performances, having a penalty – losing points for not keeping silent during someone else's presentation – usually does the trick.

Assigning roles within the group can facilitate feedback and organisation. Either the teacher or pupils themselves could decide on who takes responsibility within the group for certain tasks. Some teachers hand out badges or stick-on labels to show the pupils' roles.

For example:

- one pupil can chair or manage the group, making decisions about how to proceed

- a second can be a writer/recorder/scribe, with the job of keeping track of the work in progress and eventually the final script. Sometimes it is useful to assign this role to a pupil who would otherwise dominate the group

- a third can be the reporter/timekeeper, whose duty is to be aware of how well the group is working and to take messages to the teacher

- a fourth role, if needed, could be to back up the recorder/scribe's work.

Assessment task: end-of-unit activity

The scenario is a simulation of a television show based on a makeover: 'What not to wear'. A friend has recommended someone with a terrible wardrobe to be made over. There are two critics, one victim, and if necessary, the friend. The victim gets to select a new wardrobe based on advice received. Pupils (in role) should be encouraged to say as much as they can about what they like or don't like.

Suggested assessment criteria (for consideration by pupils)

Your result will be the average of the marks awarded by all the other groups, plus the teacher. You are aiming for:

- clear, audible speech with your best French accent

- dramatic interest (for example, surprising changes of attitude, suspense, displays of emotion, humour)

- as few breaks in your delivery and presentation as possible, showing off your good teamwork

- quality before quantity, but quality and quantity would be best of all.

It may be possible to collect a bag of jumble sale clothes to use for the 'before' and 'after' scenes. The 'after' wardrobe does not have to be better – it could be worse!

It may be possible to record the performances to allow for teachers to illustrate feedback on specific points – so that pupils can build on what they have learned when they next perform. A classroom assistant or FLA may be able to help.

From *Meeting the Needs of Your Most Able Pupils: Modern Foreign Languages*, Routledge 2008

Lesson to revise past tense formation – notes

This lesson could be used with a very able Year 9 group that is taking GCSE early and has already reached a high level, or for Year 10–11 pupils. Exceptionally able or bilingual pupils may already be able to form verbs accurately in speaking, but not necessarily in writing. Their target could be to identify the weakest links in the decision-making chain (for them) so as to be able to carry out a systematic check on their verbs and thereby improve their accuracy in writing.

Framework objectives – as an example, Key Stage 3 Year 9 objectives are included in the plan although the lesson is more likely to be used in Key Stage 4.

Follow-up

A selection of aids produced, put on display, can be referred to in future lessons – and possibly extended.

This exercise could be made the subject of a competition across several year groups. The revision aids produced could be displayed and voted on by all the pupils who have reached a suitable level of proficiency in writing and understanding grammatical terminology. Pupils need to think about their presentation and how to motivate other pupils.

 From *Meeting the Needs of Your Most Able Pupils: Modern Foreign Languages*, Routledge 2008

Lesson to revise past tense formation

French: High ability Year 9 (accelerated group), Year 10 or Year 11

Framework Objectives based on Year 9

9W5 To secure regular present tense verb patterns, main past and future tenses of high-frequency verbs, and some conditional examples.

Context of lesson

Pupils already know about formation of past tenses, know the auxiliary verbs (*être* and *avoir*). They are accustomed to working in groups. They have some knowledge about individual learning preferences. They do not yet have an overview of past tense formation.

Learning outcomes

Pupils will have applied their analytical skills. They will have a clearer view of the process of writing in the past tense. They will have designed a revision aid tailored to individual learning styles, which they will finish as homework.

Resources

Printout (or other format) of starter activity: matching relevant grammar terms and giving examples.

A starter activity

For use as a set of printed cards, a printed handout, an OHT; with a PowerPoint presentation, or an interactive whiteboard.

Pupils complete the table of grammar terms (English-French), if possible using only the French. They provide examples, then compare their ideas with others. For differentiation, other versions could be made:

● with the English equivalents missing

● with some examples included.

This table can be adapted for certain languages other than French.

anglais	français	exemple
to agree with . . . in . . .	s'accorder avec . . . en . . .	
agreement	accord	
impersonal verb	verbe impersonnel	
modal verb	auxiliaire modal	
infinitive	infinitif	
pronoun	pronom	
verb	verbe	
participle	participe	
auxiliary	auxiliaire	
past	passé	
singular	singulier	
plural	pluriel	
number	nombre	
gender	genre	
regular verb	verbe régulier	
irregular verb	verbe irrégulier	
object pronoun	pronom objet	
to agree in person (noun-verb relationship)	s'accorder en personne	
subject	sujet	
negative	négatif	

B Learning outcomes explained to pupils

The teacher states these in the TL, then asks questions (in English, if necessary) to see how much has been understood:

Today we're going to get a clear overview of how to form a range of past tenses. You're going to use your analytical skills to look at the whole process of using verbs accurately in writing and speaking. Then you are going to work together to design a customised revision aid, which you will finish as homework.

C Teaching sequence

1. Teacher models examples of verbs (mostly selected from list of frequently occurring words in the language) and elicits what is known about them, using terms covered in the starter activity. Questions should be as open as possible, should be directed at particular pupils, with pauses for pupils to listen to and consider others' responses and whether they agree or disagree.

> *j'ai dit*
>
> *j'ai lavé*
>
> *je me suis lavé(e)*
>
> *je suis allé(e)*
>
> Pupils transform these using *elles . . .*

2. As soon as possible, the teacher sets the first part of the task: working with a partner or in a small group, pupils are to analyse in English the information they need and the decisions they make as they construct the verb in the TL. The assumption is that they are working from English to the TL, i.e. translating. They are to represent the sequence of decisions initially as a rough flow chart. They can use questions if they wish.

3. The teacher circulates and assesses how pupils are progressing. Pupils can compare their versions with other groups.

4. The teacher sets the second part of the task: to represent the decision-making process as a revision aid, to suit a particular learning style. Pupils choose the style: visual, auditory, verbal, kinaesthetic, musical, interpersonal, intrapersonal. They can write, for example, a series of questions and answers; a series of rules for a game; design a poster of a (verb) tree with large and small branches, leaves, etc.; produce a comic strip or a comical role-play where one character always thinks she gets it but has to be corrected by the other.

5. Extension: groups that are working quickly can extend their 'map' to include the imperfect and future tenses plus the pluperfect, if it has been covered, and the conditional.

D Plenary

This could be conducted by one pupil, until the sequence of decisions is agreed on. Ask pupils if they have a clearer view of the process of writing in the past tense. Ask to what extent the starter activity contributed to their thinking. Ask them to share their ideas for their revision aid and whether they enjoyed the lesson.

E Homework

The teacher can calibrate the task to suit the needs of the class. If pupils are approaching examination deadlines, the idea will be to complete a finished version (tasks 4–5 above), either an accurate working diagram or flow chart, as quickly as possible. Marking criteria can be tailored to suit: if there is time to make the product more 'finished', the class and teacher need to discuss suitable criteria.

 From *Meeting the Needs of Your Most Able Pupils: Modern Foreign Languages*, Routledge 2008

Lesson to build listening skills – notes

This lesson could be used with a very able Year 9 group that is taking GCSE early and has already reached a high level, or for Year 10–11 pupils.

Framework objectives – as an example, Key Stage 3 Year 9 objectives are included in the plan although the lesson is more likely to be used in Key Stage 4.

Teaching sequence

There is a long list of varied activities. The teacher can choose to divide these up and assign different activities to different groups, or let groups choose from the menu of activities.

The strongest idea of this plan is to alternate between close study of the language and learning to listen for detail in an analytical way. It is best to use as much of the lesson time on those complementary activities. If the transcription is too awkward to handle for a large group, it could be done with individual listening stations while other activities are carried on. A good alternative is to display the text, read through it aloud as a group, while making the text disappear, until only the beginning of the line is left (as described in (1) homework).

If the teacher circulates around the class, assessing how pupils are doing, s/he can prompt, adjust plans and pace as necessary.

The other activities – comprehension, speculation and practice writing – make up the 'extension' part of the plan.

Follow-up

Much of the homework could be read out in class.

Get feedback from pupils to see how much of the song they recall, with and without prompts. A wealth of language points can be made with this material. A follow-up lesson could deal with some of those points. The teacher could model some writing by taking the point of view of the deserted wife to re-tell the story.

From *Meeting the Needs of Your Most Able Pupils: Modern Foreign Languages*, Routledge 2008

Lesson to build listening skills, while also using higher order thinking skills

French: High ability Year 9 (accelerated group), Year 10 or Year 11

Framework objectives based on Year 9

9W5 To secure regular present tense verb patterns, main past and future tenses of high-frequency verbs, and some conditional examples

9S1 That emphasis in a sentence can be changed by positioning words, phrases and clauses

9S3 How verbs work together in different tenses to extend meaning

9L1 To begin to interpret what they hear from content and tone and listen for inferences

9L3 How to report or paraphrase what they hear

9T5 Begin writing creatively

9C2 Meet the work of some famous figures in the artistic and cultural life of the country

Context of lesson

Pupils already know about formation of the present, perfect, imperfect and future tenses; they can understand and form the conditional and have occasionally met the subjunctive.

Learning outcomes

Pupils will have heard a famous French song. They will have practised their listening skills, practised reading aloud and used some complex verb patterns as models for their own writing (synthesising). They will also have analysed the ideas, meaning and effect of the song.

Links

History and citizenship (deserters and duty to one's country), literacy (language analysis and synthesis).

Resources

- Recording and complete tapescript of '*Le Déserteur*' (words by Boris Vian; music by Harold Berg and Boris Vian). These are easily found on the internet.

- Pupil's instruction sheet/exercises, pre-prepared

- Version of complete tapescript (for use on OHT or interactive whiteboard)

- Version of tapescript with all the verbs missing

- Tape/CD player

- Display of a list of instructions involving higher order thinking skills:

  Comparez, faites une synthèse, faites un résumé, faites une prédiction, montrez la différence entre, rappelez, composez un argument, analysez, persuadez.

  (The above are instructions for: comparing, synthesising, summarising, predicting, differentiating, recalling, arguing, analysing, persuading.)

Lesson to build listening skills: starter activity

A Associations

Regardez les mots suivants. Ils vous font penser à quoi? Cherchez dans le dictionnaire, si c'est nécessaire.

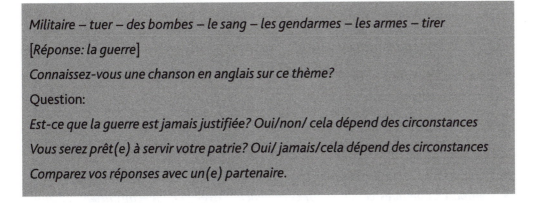

Militaire – tuer – des bombes – le sang – les gendarmes – les armes – tirer

[*Réponse: la guerre*]

Connaissez-vous une chanson en anglais sur ce thème?

Question:

Est-ce que la guerre est jamais justifiée? Oui/non/ cela dépend des circonstances

Vous serez prêt(e) à servir votre patrie? Oui/ jamais/cela dépend des circonstances

Comparez vos réponses avec un(e) partenaire.

B Learning outcomes explained to pupils

Preferably, the teacher states these in the TL, then asks questions to see how much has been understood.

'Today we're going to listen to a famous French song. You're going to use your listening skills, then select various pieces of information to prove a point.

We're also going to look at how the language in the song goes together to tell a story, so that we can use some of it to model our own writing.

Finally, we're going to see how we can build this language into our long-term memories for future use.'

C Teaching sequence

1. *Lisez les phrases a–e, puis écoutez la chanson.*

   Pendant que vous écoutez: décidez si ces phrases sont vraies ou fausses, et justifiez votre décision:

	V/F	la preuve
a. Cette personne est sûre que le Président va lire sa lettre.		
b. Cette personne hésite à prendre une décision.		
c. Il a des frères plus jeunes.		
d. Il est marié.		
e. Il n'a pas d'enfants.		

2. *Ecoutez une deuxième fois avec les paroles devant vous (mais sans verbes), en essayant de retrouver les verbes qui manquent. Vous pouvez écouter plusieurs fois. Comparez vos résultats avec un(e) partenaire.*

3. *Maintenant, lisez la chanson. Comparez votre version avec l'original.*

   Trouvez les expressions qui signalent le temps.

   Groupez les verbes (infinitif, présent, passé composé, imparfait, futur, conditionnel, impératif, autres).

4a. *Regardez bien et traduisez en anglais la phrase qui commence: j'ai vu mourir mon père.*

4b. *Comparez la version française avec la version anglaise de cette phrase. Composez quelques versions qui commencent avec 'j'ai vu + infinitive . . .' pour comparer avec un(e) partenaire.*

5. *Faites une liste des événements importants dans la vie de cette personne:*

   Il est né – . . . . il décide de déserter –

6. *Comment finira-t-il sa vie, à votre avis? Continuez la liste jusqu'à la fin. Prenez un point de vue optimiste ou pessimiste – puis comparez votre liste avec celle d'un(e) partenaire.*

   Si vous avez le temps . . .

7. *Lisez la chanson à haute voix* (aloud) *avec votre groupe.*

8. *Ecoutez cette chanson sans regarder les paroles et essayez de faire une transcription.*

9. *Répondez à ces questions:*

   Quels sont les sentiments de cet homme?
   Quelle est son attitude envers son passé?
   Quelle est son attitude envers les ordres qu'il vient de recevoir?
   Quel conseil donne-t-il au Président?

10. *Commentez sur les éléments de cette chanson que vous avez vus en étudiant la poésie/une chanson en anglais, par exemple: la répétition.*

D Plenary

This could be conducted either at intervals or at the end of the lesson. Each group could report their results for a certain section and see if others agree, or the teacher can monitor the groups, asking for feedback while circulating.

However, pupils should finish by reviewing which thinking skills they have used and where they have used them from the list on display, preferably in the TL:

comparing, synthesising, summarising, predicting, differentiating, recalling, arguing, analysing, persuading

Infinitive form: *Comparer, faire une synthèse, faire un résumé, faire une prédiction, montrer la différence, rappeler, composer un argument, analyser, persuader.*

E Homework/devoirs

Must do 1–3; could do one more activity:

1. *Essayez de rappeler les 4 premières phrases à partir de la première parole de chaque ligne:*

   Monsieur – je – que – si – je – mes – pour – avant – Monsieur – je – je – pour – il – ma – je

   [Gradually cover up more and more of the lines, working from right to left, while you read the poem/song out loud.]

2. *Faites la deuxième partie à partir de la liste des verbes.*

3. *Combien de variations sur ces phrases pouvez-vous composer (dans 3 minutes)?*

   a. *Je ne suis pas sur terre pour . . . (verbe)*

   b. *Si vous . . . prévenez . . . que je . . . et que . . .*

Appendix 4.6

4. *Imaginez la réponse du Président.*

> *Il est très touché: il comprend la position de son correspondant. Composez les 4 phrases principales de sa lettre.*
>
> *Composez 4 phrases pour montrer qu'il ne comprend pas du tout – il est très fâché!*
>
> *Le Président est trop occupé pour répondre lui-même. Imaginez une réponse composée par son secrétaire qui est complètement indifférent aux problèmes (4 phrases).*

5. Evaluation: *Faites des recherches sur l'internet pour trouver la version originale de cette chanson (les deux dernières lignes étaient différentes). Quelle version préférez-vous? Pourquoi?*

6. Extra: *Comparez les sentiments de cette chanson avec la chanson espagnole '¡A las Barricadas!' et avec d'autres en italien et allemand, si vous voulez. Est-ce que vous seriez inspiré(e) ou motivé(e) à lutter par ces chansons? Pourquoi (pas)?*

 From *Meeting the Needs of Your Most Able Pupils: Modern Foreign Languages*, Routledge 2008

Listening log for home study in MFL and pupil's sheet

What you need to do	Keywords	Typical practice material	Resources	Example
show understanding, explain	a range of sources: factual	news	Internet BBCi radio TV Authentik	*Education Guardian* language resources
infer		interviews	radio, TV	musicians in *Buena Vista Social Club*
summarise		documentaries		extract from documentary on over-fishing
recognise attitudes and emotions	imaginative	films	DVDs	scene from *Les 400 Coups*
		plays		
		poetry, song	A level textbook	poem: *'Le Déserteur'*
develop independent listening		what they are interested in	any recorded sources	bbc.co.uk/languages has audio with transcripts; songs & exercises

Building better listening skills – pupil's sheet

- Choose something you'd like to listen to – if it's funny or there's a mystery to it, or music with it, it will be more enjoyable and memorable.

- Try to get a feel for what you're going to listen to and think yourself into the situation. Maybe you can jot down some key vocabulary that you already know.

- To be able to 'recognise attitudes and emotions', listen for typical exclamations and patterns of intonation that would accompany humour, happiness/sadness, pleasure/anger, irony, sarcasm, surprise, boredom, indifference, fear and defiance.

- Ask yourself: 'How does this person feel and how do I know?'

- Listening to a large amount of rapidly spoken foreign language can make huge demands on your short-term memory, and cause negative feelings and stress. This is not motivating at all. Working with a study buddy might make a big difference, as sharing the load lowers the stress.

- Try to cover a range of material over a term.

- Look for material that also offers a transcript so that you can listen and read at the same time. Reinforce your skills by practising short sections aloud.

- Keep a record of any really good material you find so that your classmates can also try it. Try to assess its level of difficulty and if it's really difficult, try to say why.

From Meeting the Needs of Your Most Able Pupils: Modern Foreign Languages, Routledge 2008

Planning grid: developing excellent reading skills

What pupils need to do	Keywords	Types of material	Resources	Place in s.o.w.	Example	Help
summarise in detail	factual	formal	newspapers, magazines, Authentik		*Education Guardian* language resources	consortium working group
report and explain	complex language	official			www.europarl.eu.int/ charter Charter of Fundamental Rights of the European Union	
recognise attitudes and emotions	imaginative	plays, books				
handle information	consult a range of references	dictionary, web references	school library		exercises and quizzes on how to use mono- and bilingual dictionaries, grammar reference book	
develop independent reading and respond		things they are interested in	articles, stories, books, plays, weblogs			FLA, local university, colleagues abroad

From *Meeting the Needs of Your Most Able Pupils: Modern Foreign Languages*, Routledge 2008

Managing a group project – notes

This sheet is for pupils' use when working on a large-scale self-directed group project, for example, some of those mentioned in Chapter 4 as enrichment activities. It could be used when pupils from different year groups or different sets are working on a joint project, some of the time in class and some outside class time. The idea is to give pupils responsibility for managing a project, as well as helping associated members of staff (including the FLA and/or librarian) to monitor its progress and see where to give support.

- A school newspaper with articles in all the school languages, including community languages

- A school radio broadcast, podcast or video

- Planning, cooking and eating a French meal

- Internet clubs, where pupils can carry out research using online sources and work together on producing news bulletins, cultural reports, sports reports and so on

- Staging a play or a cultural evening

 From *Meeting the Needs of Your Most Able Pupils: Modern Foreign Languages*, Routledge 2008

Managing a group project – pupil's sheet

Here are some guidelines and things to consider while working through this project.

Name of project

Team members

Head of team

Goal (what you are going to do?)
Be as specific as you can: how many pages? how many items? . . .

Time frame (when will you finish?)
Do you need to overestimate how long it will take just in case?

Suggested steps:

- define your goals

- break into separate tasks or activities

- consider your resources – look at the time available; don't be over-optimistic

- build in some back-up – team members supporting each other; outside support

- develop a schedule – estimate timing and what needs to be done first

- do the work

- put it together

- complete

- assess your performance – what has been learnt?

Diary of Meetings

Date	Action agreed	Who?	When?

After the project is finished

What did you learn from this project?

Consider what you got out of this project. Researchers think that this sort of work develops certain abilities in pupils. These are listed below. What do you think? Did this project bring out abilities in you?

How did it show your:

independence (give an example)

critical thinking

creative thinking

problem-solving ability

reflecting

motivation?

Did you learn anything about yourself (your qualities and strengths) that surprised you?

Help from other people:

Librarian

Class teacher

Languages assistant

IT teacher

Others

What suggestions would you make to another group of pupils who are planning to do a similar project?

 From *Meeting the Needs of Your Most Able Pupils: Modern Foreign Languages*, Routledge 2008

Revision mind map on 'my region' in Spanish

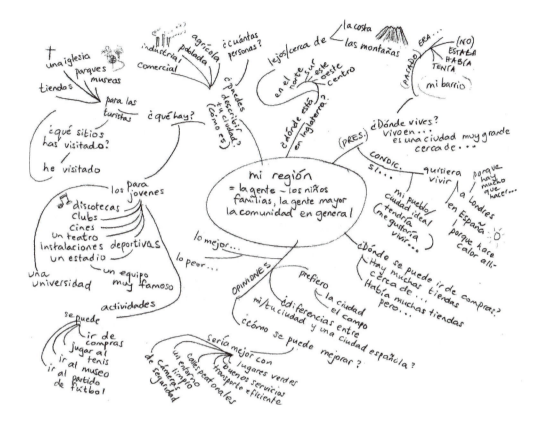

Revision mind map on 'food' in Italian

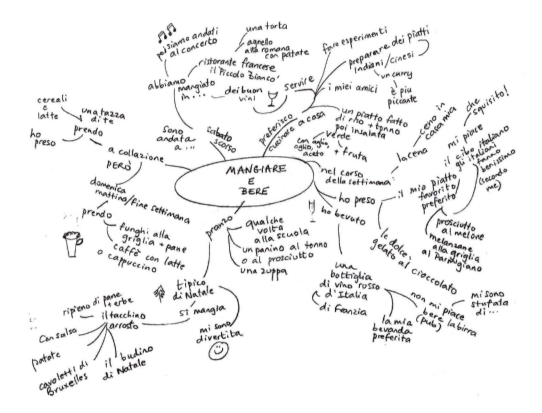

 From *Meeting the Needs of Your Most Able Pupils: Modern Foreign Languages*, Routledge 2008

Role of the foreign language assistant

The foreign language assistant (FLA) is

- a source of information about the country and the language

- an integrated member of a language teaching team.

General principles

The FLA and teacher work in partnership on themes, oral exercises, comprehension exercises, games, etc.

The FLA must use the target language as continuously as possible, particularly with older students – a careful look at the textbook will guide the FLA as to how much students know and which words to use.

The FLA must:

- with help from staff – become familiar with the demands of exams and the types of practice required

- maintain communication with staff over lessons and pupils' progress

- provide reassurance and encouragement for students – keeping in mind that a difference in standards or emphasis in different countries does not imply better or worse

- provide oral work at the appropriate level (with guidance from staff) using as sources the widest possible variety: radio, video, magazines, advertisements, newspapers, games, postcards, labels, etc.

- provide help and guidance to staff in the form of discussion and provision of vocabulary for FL essays

- whether doing individual or small-group work, try to provide individual attention and foster a relaxed atmosphere.

Nature of work

No marking of written work is ever required. Depending on the timetable or needs of specific pupils or groups, work will consist of:

- conversation lessons with small groups of A level students: topics under guidance of A level staff. Preparation is required but no marking

- practice of GCSE language with small groups of pupils: limited range of conversation topics, vocabulary and role-plays. FLA may be asked to assess students on their preparation/attainment

- support with the after-school language club, by arrangement with the supervisor

- support with individual or groups of more-able language learners

- support with vocabulary acquisition and basic language skills with children with learning difficulties (see school SEN policy)

- practice of basic role-plays and vocabulary acquisition with small groups of junior pupils – in or out of the classroom, as directed by the classroom teacher.

The languages department will provide, in addition to teacher's guidance mentioned previously:

- a full briefing on departmental resources and school/local authority resources

- some material (books and pamphlets) giving guidance and ideas on how to organise the material and the activities concerned

- photocopying of necessary materials, by arrangement with the head of department.

Recording and monitoring

The FLA will sign in and out at the office. S/he must telephone the school or the head of department if s/he is unable to come to work.

The FLA will keep a diary of each day's work, showing which group s/he worked with, which member of staff and a brief description of the activity carried out. The diary will be kept in the department. The HOD will use it to check time sheets at the end of each month.

The FLA will see the member of staff directly in charge of her/him on a regular basis – at least once every two weeks. The time will be used for planning and for the FLA to raise any concerns or problems. At the end of the academic year, the FLAs will receive a statement of when they worked at the school, signed by the head teacher, and a reference from the HOD based on the year's work.

 From *Meeting the Needs of Your Most Able Pupils: Modern Foreign Languages*, Routledge 2008

References

Balmer, S. (2002) 'Gosforth High School: fast track French group' CILT-SLC case study. CILT, The National Centre for Languages. 7 November 2005. www.cilt.org.uk/languagecolleges/enrichment/gosforth.htm.

Bloom, B. (1956) *Taxonomy of Educational Objectives.* London: Methuen.

CILT (1999) *Learning through a foreign language: models, methods and outcomes.*

Clark, C. and Callow, R. (2002) *Educating the Gifted and Talented: Resource Issues and Processes for Teachers.* London: David Fulton Publishers.

DfES (1998) *Extending opportunity: a national framework for study support.* London: DfES.

DfES (1998) *Circular to Headteachers and Teachers: Reducing the Bureaucratic Burden on Teachers* circular 2/98. London: DfES.

DfES (2001) *Schools Achieving Success.* London: HMSO.

DfES (2001) *Nord Anglia Research Project for DfES – May 2001.* 24 October 2005. www.standards.dfes.gov.uk/giftedandtalented/downloads/word/nordangliaresearchproject.doc.

DfES (2001) *Study Support in Teacher Training and Professional Development* (DfES 0492/2001).

DfES (2002) *KS3 National Strategy.* DfES 0382/2002.

DfES/QCA (1997) *Modern Foreign Languages in the National Curriculum: Managing the Programmes of Study Part I: learning and using the target language.* QCA publications.

DfES/QCA (1998) *Modern Foreign Languages in the National Curriculum: Managing the Areas of Experience Programmes of Study part II: areas of experience.* QCA publications.

DfES/QCA (1999) *National Curriculum for MFL.* HMSO.

DfES/QCA (1999) *National Curriculum Handbook for Secondary Teachers in England & Wales.* HMSO.

DfES/QCA (2000a) *Guidance for MFL KS3 Schemes of Work.* HMSO.

DfES/QCA (2000b) *National Literacy Strategy.* DfES/QCA.

DfES/QCA (2001) *Optional Tests and Tasks MFL (update).* QCA.

Eyre, D. (1997) *Able Children in Ordinary Schools.* London: David Fulton Publishers.

Eyre, D. and Lowe, H. (2002) *Curriculum Provision for the Gifted and Talented in the Secondary School.* London: David Fulton Publishers.

Freeman, J. (1997) 'The Emotional development of the highly able'. *European Journal of Psychology in Education.* XII, 479–493.

Freeman, J. (1998) *The Education of the Very Able: Current International Research.* London: HMSO.

Freeman, J. (2002) 'Out-of-school Educational Provision for the Gifted and Talented Around the World'. A report to the DfES. 7 November 2005. http://www.joanfreeman.com/mainpages/freepapers.htm

Gardner, H. (1983/2003). *Frames of Mind. The theory of multiple intelligences.* New York: BasicBooks.

Gardner, H. (1997) *The First Seven Intelligences – and the Eighth: A Conversation with Howard Gardner By Kathy Checkley* 1997, The National Education Association. http://www.nea.org/teachexperience/braiko30627.html.

George, D. (1997) *The Challenge of the Able Child* 2nd edn. London: David Fulton Publishers.

Leyden, S. (1998) *Supporting the Child of Exceptional Ability: At Home and School* 2nd edn. London: David Fulton Publishers in association with The National Association for Able Children in Education.

Lightbown, P. M. and Spada, N. (1993) *How Languages are Learned.* Cambridge: CUP.

Lowe, Hilary in Eyre, D. and Lowe, H. (eds) (2002) *Curriculum Provision for the Gifted and Talented in the Secondary School.* London: David Fulton Publishers.

OCR (2000) *A MFL syllabus 2001.* OCR.

OCR (2000) *AEA MFL syllabus 2001.* OCR.

OCR (2000) *GCSE MFL syllabus 2001.* OCR.

Ofsted (2000a) *Annual Report of Her Majesty's Chief Inspector of Schools 1989/1999.* London: Ofsted.

Ofsted (2000b) *Inspecting subjects 11–16 MFL.* London: Ofsted.

Ofsted (2001) *Providing for gifted and talented pupils: an evaluation of Excellence in Cities and other grant funded programmes.* London: Ofsted.

Ofsted (2001a) *Annual Report of Her Majesty's Chief Inspector of Schools 1999–2000.* London: Ofsted

Ofsted (2001b) *Subject Reports: Secondary Modern Foreign Languages.* London: Ofsted.

Renzulli, J. S. (1997) 'What Makes Giftedness? Re-examining a Definition.' *Phi Delta Kappan*, 60(3), 180–184, 261.

Riding, R. (2002) *School Learning and Cognitive Style.* London: David Fulton Publishers.

Sloan, K. and Frost, P. (2004) 'The NAGTY Summer School Programme: Life-Changing Experience for Students, active CPD for teachers, or both?' The National Academy for Gifted and Talented Youth. 4 November 2005. www.nagty.ac.uk/. . ./downloadable_materials/documents/summer_school_programme_ken_sloan_peter_frost.doc.

Vygotsky, L. S. (1978) *Mind in Society*, Cambridge, Mass.: Harvard University Press.

Willard-Holt, C. (1994) *Recognizing Talent: Cross-Case Study of Two High Potential Students With Cerebral Palsy* (CRS 94308). The National Research Center on the Gifted and Talented, University of Connecticut. 5 November, 2005. http://www.gifted.uconn.edu/nrcgt/reports/crs94308/crs94308.html.

Wragg, E.C. and Brown, G. (2001) *Questioning in the Secondary School.* London: Routledge.

Further information

Useful contacts and resources

There are innumerable organisations and resources for language teachers: this list is not exhaustive.

The websites and links existed at the time this book went to print – and were found useful. However, the author accepts no responsibility for the actual content of any materials suggested as information sources. Teachers should check all website references carefully to see if they have changed before referring pupils to them.

Organisations with websites

Advanced Placement schemes www.ap.ca

Aim Higher www.aimhigher.ac.uk

ALL Association for Language Learning. The subject association for teachers of all modern foreign languages at all levels: www.all-languages.org.uk

Becta The British Educational Communications and Technology agency. Information and communications technology (ICT) and e-learning strategy for schools and the learning and skills sectors. http://curriculum.becta.org.uk

The British Council www.britishcouncil.org

CILT The National Centre for Languages (formerly the Centre for Information on Language Teaching and Research; now merged with the Languages National Training Organisation). 20, Bedfordbury, London WC2 4LB Tel: 020 7879 5101. www.cilt.org.uk

G & T Wise support: www2.teachernet.gov.uk/gat

The International Baccalaureate www.ibo.org

InTuition Languages Ltd. www.in-languages.com

Kilve Court, Somerset www.kilvecourt.org

Linguanet ICT www.linguanet.org.uk

London Gifted & Talented www.londongt.org.

NACE www.nace.co.uk

NAGC www.nagcbritain.org.uk

The National Curriculum in Action www.ncaction.org.uk

National Curriculum Standards website www.standards.dfes.gov.uk/giftedand talented

The Open University www.open.ac.uk/yass

Oxbridge Academic Programs www.oxbridgeprograms.com

QCA-administered www.nc.uk.net/gt and www.qca.org.uk

Teacher Resource Exchange: resources and activities http://tre.ngfl.gov.uk

TES newsday www.newsday.co.uk

Theatre in education company performing in foreign languages www.onatti.co.uk

Vektor distance learning www.vektor.com

Young Gifted and Talented http://ygt.dcsf.gov.uk (formerly NAGTY)

Language link collections

Compared with only a few years ago, there are almost too many resources for language teachers available via the internet. Maintaining large link collections is becoming less common with the advent of powerful search engines. Link collections maintained by various universities are still a good starting point. Where people's names are given, they can be used as another way in to the site. See ict4lt for what to do if a link has died. The absence of a particular language from this list does not imply that the language is any less important.

www.ict4lt.org – information and communications technology for language learners: all you need to know about using the internet and languages, including links.

www.quia.com – an educational technology website

www.epals.com – a website for cross-cultural exchange

www.bbc.co.uk/languages – the BBC now has its first stand-alone courses in Spanish and French

www.authentik.com Authentik – magazines and audio in a range of languages

www.linguanet.org.uk Linguanet – UK resource site for modern languages

www.ashcombe.surrey.sch.uk/Curriculum/modlang – Ashcombe Language College offers a range of languages and resources

French link resources

http://hapax.french.sbc.edu – page created and maintained by Angelo Metzidakis

www.utm.edu/departments/french/french.html – Tennessee Bob's Famous French Links

Italian link resources

www.cyberitalian.com

Spanish link resources

www.studyspanish.com

German link resources

www.swan.ac.uk/german/links.htm – Swansea University's list of resources for German teachers and students

www.deutsch-online.com

www.goethe.de – Goethe-Institut

www.uncg.edu/˜lixlpurc/german.html – maintained by Andreas Lixl-Purcell

www.isu.edu/˜nickcrai/german.html – design by Curt Nickisch

www.ualberta.ca – German and Scandinavian languages links for teachers

http://sps.k12.mo.us/khs/german/songbook/songbook.htm maintained by Brian Zahn

www.german-way.com – the German Way: culture and resources

www.acampitelli.com/links.htm – German for Music Lovers

www.germanfortravellers.com – German for Travellers

Latin

www.cambridgescp.com

Japanese

http://japanese.about.com – language-related information and fun, with links and resources for teachers (see also French.about.com, German, Spanish and Italian)